NumberWise

NumberWise

*How to Analyze Your
Facts and Figures for
Smart Business Decisions*

Michael C. Thomsett

amacom

American Management Association

This publication is designed to provide accurate and authoritative information in regard to the subject matter covered. It is sold with the understanding that the publisher is not engaged in rendering legal, accounting, or other professional service. If legal advice or other expert assistance is required, the services of a competent professional person should be sought.

Library of Congress Cataloging-in-Publication Data

Thomsett, Michael C.
    NumberWise : how to analyze your facts and figures for smart business decisions / Michael C. Thomsett.
        p: cm.
    Includes index.
    ISBN 0-8144-5038-5
    1. Corporations—Finance.   2. Decision-making.   I. Title.
    HG4011.T5   1992
658.15—dc20   91-55506
                                                                    CIP

Contents

NumberWise

Chapter 1

The Need for Analysis

Imagine a pilot, flying a plane at night without any gauges to indicate fuel level, elevation, or air speed. Where are the mountains? Where is the closest airport, and can the plane make it that far?

Just as the pilot has a critical need for gauges, business owners need to track information about the business. Without the financial facts and figures provided by accountants and analysts, the leaders of your company could not make informed decisions. They would be flying blind.

In most forms of analysis, the past is the base for projecting the future. Analysis shows you how past conditions and events turned out; and that indicates what could happen in the future. However, the purpose of analysis is not to completely remove the risk or uncertainty from estimates. This mistaken belief places a lot of pressure on everyone expected to budget, plan, or estimate the future. The real purpose of analysis is to identify probable outcomes if certain actions are taken. For example, if the company expands into a new territory, will the move have a reasonable chance of being profitable? The answer will be based on past expansion, existing competition, and a number of other factors.

MAKING YOUR POINT WITH NUMBERS

Because the world of business is oriented toward profit and loss, those who are able to communicate in terms of finance have more influence and more opportunities.

The difference between accounting and nonaccounting approaches is one of discipline. Accountants know, from the experience of working with financial information, exactly how to translate numbers into meaningful facts. They also know how to get information to the top so that informed decisions are possible.

But you don't need an accounting background in order to use the numbers to your advantage. The secret of using the numbers to your own best advantage is not in gaining skills you don't already have. The truth is, accountants have no special secrets or knowledge that you do not possess. Even as a nonaccountant manager, you already know enough to make analysis a powerful tool for communication and for gaining and exercising the influence you deserve. The secret is to learn how to use analysis as a tool for improved communication. You need to adopt a new attitude: Every issue that comes up has a profit and loss question that deserves to be answered. From this new point of view, you will also learn how to use analysis. Even a completely intangible problem does, in fact, have a profit question and answer. That's where informed analysis can become one of your strongest weapons. If you are able to communicate in terms of profits for every issue raised, you will soon be perceived as a valuable, aware member of the company team. Remember, you already know your own department better than anyone else. You are in the best position to advise top management on issues affecting you. Now, you need to apply your expertise in another forum: profitability. You need to make the transition from a non-numbers manager to a well-rounded manager who knows both the human and the profit side of every issue.

TWO SIDES TO THE BOTTOM LINE

The art of financial analysis involves values: dollars and cents, production volume, numbers of employees, sales calls, customers signed up, and so forth.

Top management seems obsessed with the bottom line. It examines every issue and considers every decision by asking, "Will it be profitable?" or "How much will it cost?"

You cannot be right about the future; you can only support a well-conceived estimate. Too often, managers feel pressured to be right in their estimates—an unreasonable position. When you are dealing with the future, your analysis is supportable as long as you have developed it by labeling assumptions, carrying the right information through to a logical conclusion, and identifying the related risks along the way.

Asking questions is management's job. Management is responsible for enacting the agenda imposed by the owners. This usually includes generating a profit. So management on all levels has an obligation to the company: to maximize profits and reduce costs and expenses. Even if you find the profit issue distasteful, remember that without it, the company wouldn't exist and you wouldn't have a job.

This is the financial side of the picture. But there's another side as well—the human side. Many decades ago, employees were viewed as a commodity. Supply and demand determined their wages, and companies were not responsible beyond that. In the more enlightened modern company, management has come to recognize that hiring employees involves an obligation in human terms, and not just in terms of salary and benefits. The company needs to ensure that the working environment is safe and secure, that employees are given what they need to perform their jobs, and that they have a fair opportunity to advance in their careers.

Virtually every informed management scientist will agree that when the human side works well, the bottom line is enhanced. A motivated, satisfied staff is the backbone of *permanent* growth. When turnover is high and employees are exploited and treated poorly, the company's profitability inevitably declines. It is rarely coincidental. There is a direct and recognizable link between employee morale and profit.

This human side of the bottom line is the side you, as a nonaccounting manager, work with constantly. But remember, it's all the same. The human issues you confront also affect the bottom line. You cannot separate financial and human issues and treat them differently. To communicate with top management effectively, you need to express yourself in financial terms, even when the issue on the table seems to have nothing to do with finance. Remember the executive's obsession: profit and loss. If you enter a meeting with a request relating to a human issue, and if you express that issue in human terms, you miss an opportunity to communicate well. You will do much better if you are able to express your human issue in the financial terms the decision maker expects.

Here's the key: *Every* issue has a financial side. Your goal is—or should be—to become a skilled analyst, one who is able to take a nonfinancial issue, study it, understand the financial ramifications (even the intangible ones), and then present your case in financial terms.

THE FINANCIAL SIDE OF A NONFINANCIAL PROBLEM

Translating pure numbers into meaningful facts, information, and solutions is obviously not easy. Perhaps the most challenging concept within that exercise is finding the clearest and most applicable financial expression of a nonfinancial idea. This is the task you, a nonaccountant manager, will confront every day.

Let's see how the process might work.

You suggested to management that your department be relocated one floor down. The reason: Most of your work involves interaction with departments on the other floor. The move is estimated to cost $4,000 and will involve two to three days of down time. Your idea was rejected: too expensive. You believe that, if the issue could be converted to financial terms, you could prove it makes sense.

You decide you will try to estimate the degree of wasted time associated with travel from one department to another. The wasted time certainly has a financial value, and a brief study could establish the probable benefits in terms of dollars and cents. Think through the elements that might go into your study:

- The number of trips between departments per day.
- The average amount of time involved in going from one location to another.
- An estimate of idle time while employees are not within view of their immediate supervisor.
- Any other factors associated with the inefficiency of operating on two separate floors: This may involve use of equipment in another department, loss of productivity due to poor communication, and the need to add processing steps consequential to distance.

All these factors, added together, can then be assigned a fair dollar value. Now relate that to the dollar value of payroll costs of employees in your department (salary plus benefits). With the nonfinancial issue reduced to a dollar amount, you can calculate how much time is required to recapture the initial cost of the move and clearly demonstrate that after the recapture time, you will be operating at a lower cost.

If you manage a department that does not deal with the customer directly (and most don't), you might well ask, "How can I generate a profit in the department?" Every department has a bottom line, although finding it may take a new perspective. For the nonaccounting manager, the bottom line might be related to productivity, accuracy or error rate, or meeting a deadline. It might be improving operating systems, beating a budget, or putting together a successful project team.

Forget for the moment the idea that a "profit" necessarily has to be a financial result. Because most departments deal not with dollars and cents, but with some other commodity (service, information, support), the very idea of profit needs to be redefined. So a bottom line in your department might be defined as a nonfinancial result such as information. You "profit" by supplying valuable information when it is needed.

Example: The marketing director in your company puts together a monthly sales summary, based on information you compile and organize into a report. If that information is supplied in a timely manner, the marketing director can work with various sales offices to identify opportunities. However, if the information arrives too far into the month, the opportunities are lost.

In this example, the "profit" potential is derived from receiving the information in a timely manner. Just as dollar profits are essential to keep the whole company running, information profits help to create and take advantage of opportunities in the field, in another department, or in the boardroom.

TECHNIQUES FOR DEFINING PROBLEMS

In the real world, the difficult part of analysis is not working with a neatly defined situation. Most of the time, you first have to find the elements of the problem, define it, and *then* figure out how to solve it. By the time you get around to actually doing the analysis, most of the work has already been done. Developing problem-solving techniques on your own is an essential part of the analysis procedure. Here are some guidelines for defining problems.

• **Consult with everyone who is involved.** The definition of problems depends more than anything else on discussing the relevant issues with everyone who is involved. And that means all those who are affected—people in other departments, the decision makers, and even your own employees. The greater the degree of appropriate participation, the better.

One danger of consultation at length is that you will spend all your time in discussions. At some point, you need to end the discussions and act. So it helps if you set a deadline for beginning your solution. Advertise the deadline. Hold a meeting. Advise and ask for ideas and suggestions. Then respond to whatever is said. But once the deadline is upon you, act. The time for talking will have passed.

• **Remain open-minded.** Sometimes, you secretly think you already understand the problem thoroughly; you think you're involving others but in reality you're only going through the motions. This is a dangerous move. People see through it, and lose respect for those who practice it. Always be willing to look at a different point of view, and to abandon your own ideas if they end up being wrong. A lot of time is wasted in struggling just to hold onto an idea that is simply wrong.

• **Test continuously, and be willing to change your course when necessary.** Your analysis depends on theories continuing to hold true. For example, you might take great pains to define a problem and arrive at an entirely appropriate solution through analysis. However, some months later, that procedure could be obsolete. Be willing to abandon old ideas that no longer work.

• **Remember, the same rules don't always apply.** If you truly want to become a talented problem solver, don't assume that the same techniques work in every situation. Don't become a "one-solution manager." Some people fall into the trap of finding one thing that works, and then trying to apply that to everything they encounter. Be aware that every problem demands a new solution. While some of the things you learn through experience will certainly apply in new situations, you also need to keep an open mind to other possibilities.

THE DIFFICULT PART OF ANALYSIS

The *easy* part of analysis is manipulating the numbers. They can be averaged, expressed as ratios, placed on a chart, or made into color slides for a dazzling presentation at the board of directors meeting. But these reporting techniques are the end results. Before that can happen, you have to go through the *difficult* part.

You first need to make sure you have the right numbers.

Obvious? Of course it is, but so few people take this critical step. They understand where some information resides, and they might even know how to translate it into a well-expressed trend. But there are other, more important questions to always ask first, if only to ensure that you are proceeding correctly.

The first question is, What problem am I trying to solve? Solutions are wonderful things, especially those that present themselves easily. But realistically, we all know that solutions do not always address the problems at hand. The wise business professional is careful to define problems before rushing to solutions.

Next ask yourself, Does the information I'm planning to use actually point a way to a solution? If you're just stirring information around without arriving at a useful end result, then the analysis is worthless.

Finally, ask yourself, What additional information might be more revealing? It's human nature to restrict ourselves to what is familiar and easy to obtain. But sometimes, information held by someone else is more relevant to the problem you're trying to solve. Look around. Who else could supply you with useful information? Another department? Other files within your own control? Look for the most relevant, rather than the most convenient.

DEFINING THE PROBLEM

It seems obvious that the first step is to define a problem, and *then* come up with a solution. But many people, thinking of themselves as action oriented, rush to solutions as quickly as possible, even before knowing what needs fixing. Aim to become the type of analytical problem solver who develops trends *after* defining problems and getting others to validate your conclusion. Once everyone agrees what the problem is, a solution is much easier to put into action.

This requires dialogue between departments and between managers. You need to ensure that your agenda is the same as the agenda of the executive who gave you the assignment; or that the departmental problem you are solving for yourself has interest to other managers.

Defining the problem is not as simple as sitting down with a group of others and discussing the issues at hand. You probably already know that people can discuss the same issue with entirely different agendas in mind, or use the same wording but with different meanings. The communication problem is compounded because all participants in that communication have a perspective that is unique to them, their department, and the sum of their own background and experience. Be aware at all times of this key point:

> The other person sees the issues in an entirely different way than you do.

Protect yourself by making every effort to define the problem being addressed in your trend analysis. Take all the steps you can to communicate the defined problem to others clearly, and to invite constructive dialogue. There is no crime in struggling to gain agreement. The problems arise when you proceed without first trying to explain your approach to other people.

INTERNAL MARKETING

The manager of a back-office department never sees a customer in the traditional sense of the word. But in fact, the manager of every department has a customer and serves that customer every day. Accounting departments, for example, deliver products (reports, paychecks, statements) and services (consultation, budgetary advice, auditing) to other departments. Remember this key point:

> Every department has a bottom line, and every function has a customer.

When a marketing person begins his or her task, the first step is to define the customer and the product. Without those two elements clearly understood, it would be impossible to sell. The successful marketing plan is based on the idea of knowing what the customer wants, and then delivering it. The same is true when you take the approach that you have both a bottom line and a customer.

If your department, like most, delivers something of value to another department rather than directly to the external customer, then you do have a product and your functions serve a customer's needs. The definition is probably quite easy. Who needs the information or other services you provide? The answer will define your customer. And the "product" you deliver is just as important as the product delivered to the external customer. There is a demand, and your department is there to respond to it.

So it is fairly easy to see how the accounting department might be market-driven. Everyone in the company is a customer, since they are all on the payroll, and they all need information. Now let's examine a few other departments and see how they might also take on a market-driven feature. The personnel department provides employee support, organizes and administers benefits, mediates disputes and grievances, takes care of compliance, and manages hiring and terminations. That's a lot, and it involves a number of customers. The many products we have listed are essential in the employee community of the company.

Another department worth looking at as market-driven is a processing area. For example, some organizations have word processing pools, claims departments, or other groups that handle a number of transactions each day. In this case, the product is a tangible one. The processed transaction is a parallel to the product manufactured from raw materials in a productivity environment. The customer is the department that receives the processed transaction, or it could be the external customer.

Example: A service department deals directly with the external customer after the sale has been made. The contact may be months or even years later. However, prompt and professional service creates long-standing customer loyalty. With that in mind, the "product" is of extreme importance and value to the customer; it leads to future sales.

Example: You manage an insurance claims processing department. You have noticed that when volume is heavy, employees tend to make more errors. Your attitude is that everything sent out of the department is a product, and everyone who receives something is a customer. As part of your "customer service" program, you take steps to reduce the error rate.

Your goal must be: Create in your department an environment that can be analyzed in the same tangible way as an external market. Seeing your department as a "market-driven" center changes your attitude and your approach to problems. When you gear your thinking toward the customer and the bottom line, you sharpen your management approach. In the sense that you offer the equivalent of product or service to other departments, you must be able to generate profits and maintain them—just as the marketing department must find ways to sell to the external market at a net profit.

When you begin thinking of yourself as the manager of a department that provides internal marketing services, you will find analysis is easier. You will be able to analyze seemingly intangible factors and arrive at a tangible, financial reference. This makes it possible to present information and requests to the decision maker with much greater clarity.

To summarize, your challenge is to employ marketing techniques *and* accounting skills to improve your influence within the organization. You will translate these skills into the analysis—on a financial level—of issues you face every day. Your point of view will become extremely financial, even though your motive may be entirely human.

THE SECRET TO GETTING A "YES"

Many nonaccounting managers go into meetings and present problems to decision makers. They say, in effect, here's my problem; solve it for me. In contrast, a few people have learned the big secret of getting things done their way. They offer answers rather than questions. Before the decision maker has a chance to ask the questions—How much profit is involved? What is this going to cost?—these people have already prepared the answers.

For example, suppose you want to hire another person in your department. Your employees are buried in work, putting in overtime, and making more errors each month. Your workload is tied directly to sales volume, and this year's forecast predicts yet another growth spurt.

You could go into a budget meeting and insist on a larger payroll budget, arguing: We're so busy, work quality is dropping, and we need more help. But these are complaints, problems begging a solution.

Now consider the alternative: You go into the meeting with a study of two factors: overtime costs and error rates. Your study shows that error rates will be reduced if workload is lessened. It also shows that hiring one additional full-time employee will save overtime costs.

Decision makers are far more likely to approve requests from someone who has done all the work—before even coming to the meeting. If you want others to approve your requests, be prepared to offer valid information that proves your point. Show why a positive decision is profitable *and* contains no risk, and you will get the approval you want every time.

A profitable outcome is any condition that reduces costs or expenses, or directly improves the bottom line. Whenever an idea achieves any of these advantages, you should make this extremely clear in your presentation. In fact, whenever you make a request for a change, always look for a way to express your request in terms of a bottom-line solution.

The second point worth demonstrating to decision makers is that there is little or no risk involved with saying yes. The way to do this is with analysis of historical information to estimate outcomes in the future. Take great care to not overstate your case. Remember that forecasts are nothing more than estimates. You cannot guarantee a no-risk outcome; you can only use past information to support your point that the risks are not excessive.

Decision makers are likely to respond well when you approach them with the two-point program. Remember, decision makers are only human. They will respond better to managers who make their jobs easier.

As valuable as historical information is, there are limitations to its use. Most executive decision makers are oriented toward action. They will expect you to look to the future more than to the past.

Chapter 2

Finding Dependable Information

In business situations, we often confront moments in which information is used in questionable ways. There are so many possible interpretations of the same sets of raw data that any number of results could be possible. How do you know whether you're interpreting information correctly? And how do you know whether you have the *right* information to begin with?

HISTORICAL INFORMATION

The most commonly used type of information, and one of the most dependable, is historical. This is true in both financial and nonfinancial cases. In the financial situation, the advantages of historical data are well understood. For example, an accountant will develop and track a series of ratios and, from that, report a number of trends. When current results exceed what management considers an acceptable ratio, action is taken to put the trend back on an acceptable course. This is a perfectly appropriate use of historical information. It typifies the basic analysis that accountants and other financially oriented managers and employees perform routinely.

You may find similar applications in your own department. Historical information is all around you. Your department's budget is one form of historical financial information. Some data will be nonfinancial. For example, your employees have executed a specific number of transactions, worked varying numbers of hours, or used an office machine at an increasing rate over the past year. All these historical facts can be accumulated, organized, and used in requests, analysis, future budgets, and reports you generate.

However, remember:

> It's a mistake to take too much comfort in consistency, especially at the expense of accuracy.

Historically based information may not serve your purpose completely. In many situations, an analysis may need to combine historical with other forms of data. Assuming that your analysis will be reviewed, perhaps even challenged, by others will help you to develop valid arguments and explanations. This is the ultimate test of analysis, even when no one else will ever see it. Would you be able to support your conclusions if discussing them with someone else? How did you define and then collect your raw information? How was your analysis developed? Was it manipulated to create the outcome you wanted? Or did you test and question it to ensure that your study was fair and objective?

It's a good idea to build a source file of recurring factors in your department. You probably need to develop your source file over a number of months. Correctly developed, this file can become a valuable collection of intelligence, to be used later in many ways.

Example: The manager of a data processing department observed that the company's mainframe computer was accessed very infrequently during the morning hours but quite heavily in the afternoon, creating a serious bottleneck. He has an idea for improving the situation, but first he tracks terminal access trends for three months. At the end of that time, he suggests that the accounting department input its daily transaction batch at 8 A.M. for the previous day, rather than at 4 P.M. At first the accounting manager resists: "We always cut off on the day the work was transacted. We can't change that." However, when the data processing manager presents his three-month analysis of access trends, the accounting manager changes his mind and accepts the recommendation.

Example: You prepare a brief report documenting the need for two additional input terminals in your department. Your case is built around workload growth during the last two years. Without any staff increases, you have experienced a 35 percent increase in the volume of work.

This is an impressive fact, and it may support your request quite well. But to make your case stronger, you supply additional information: current purchase or lease prices of terminals; a summary of the current year's sales forecast, which supports your contention that departmental volume will continue to grow; and a projection of the employee time savings you will achieve with the additional terminals in place.

In an ironic way, the historical emphasis practiced by the accounting profession is both an advantage and a hindrance— especially when the company's leadership is keenly focused on marketing. Expanding markets is the extreme expression of looking to the future.

DANGERS OF INVALID DATA

No matter how good an analyst you become, your reports will be completely wrong if you use erroneous information or interpret information incorrectly. No matter how much time and effort you put into developing a message, if your premise is based on the wrong information, the entire exercise is a waste of time.

How can you recognize invalid data or, more to the point, what do you need to do to verify the information you plan to use? You will certainly run into situations in which you do misinterpret information, draw the wrong conclusion, and make mistakes. That happens to everyone who performs analysis. You will also run into cases where your approach seems to make sense, but someone else sees the numbers as having an entirely different meaning. In those cases, no one is absolutely right; it's a matter of opinion.

> *Example:* The accounting department recommended curtailing a requested budget increase for one department. The reason: Requested new spending would be about 30 percent higher than the previous year, and last year's budget represented a similar change from the year before. On the surface, it looked as though too much money was being spent and better controls were needed.
>
> However, the department's manager demonstrated that the requested increases were, in fact, a *reduction* in departmental spending, even though the money amount was higher. Staff increases as well as transaction load in the department had grown by more than 50 percent per year. It was only with tight, direct control systems that the manager had been able to keep spending down to its historical level and was able to request *only* a 30 percent increase for the following year.

In this example, the accountant's observation was entirely proper. The numbers did show spending growing at a fast rate for the department. However, on further examination, it became apparent that the department's manager was doing a superb job of keeping expenses down and even reducing the per-transaction cost of running the department.

The problem here is not just the consequence of a difference of opinion. The accountant simply didn't have access to the information needed to interpret the situation accurately.

How do you protect yourself against a well-meaning but inaccurate interpretation? Arm yourself with facts and go to meetings prepared, as did the manager in the example above.

VALIDATING THE RATIO

In many companies and departments today, invalid analysis is being cheerfully performed but never checked. Why? Because there is no means for finding out that the analysis is misguided. No one ever acts on discovered information coming from the analysis. If no one responds, what is the point of doing an analysis and discovering that something is wrong? A key point:

> The analysis is worth doing only if you and others are able to act in response to what you discover.

The response is where you discover whether or not your analysis has any merit. If your analysis shows a negative trend and you take action to correct it, you would expect to see results. However, if those results don't occur, either the action you selected was ineffective, or the trend itself is not accurate.

If you are asked to perform an analysis, especially one that is part of a recurring routine, but no one ever acts on what it reveals, resist doing the task. It's a waste of time. You might not have the power to simply refuse, but there are a number of steps you can take:

1. *Eliminate the work itself.* Suggest cancelling the routine. There is no value to creating important information no one uses.
2. *Recommend the appropriate actions.* Suggest actions others might take. Point out the problem: The information is important, but no one is acting on it. One way out is to suggest ways the problem can be solved.
3. *Take over and do what's needed.* Volunteer to take the actions yourself. If no one else wants to do anything in response to what your analysis reveals, take on the job yourself.
4. *Reduce the time commitment.* Suggest completing the task quarterly instead of monthly. This at least reduces your wasted time by two-thirds. If you can't com-

pletely eliminate a useless task, at least do it as little as possible.

After an analysis has been done several times, you will be able to audit your work. Ask yourself: Do the trends reveal what we're looking for? Are the ratios clear and do they convey information to others? If not, how can they be changed or replaced?

To validate the trend, check indicated actions against the trend itself. Do you see a change in direction as the result of changes you have prompted?

Example: You prepare a monthly trend report in which you analyze the time required to collect money from customers. Several months ago, the average number of days required began rising. You suggested a few changes in collection policies, which were put into effect at that time.

The validation process can now be undertaken. Did the changes you suggested reverse the emerging negative trend? Did the number of days required to collect outstanding accounts decline and stabilize? If they did, it indicates that the ratio is valid, that it does give you valuable information.

You will notice, however, that validation can only occur if actions are taken in response to what the ratio shows. If there is no response, there can be no validation. A lack of response validates only one thing: that the analysis itself is a waste of time and will continue to be unless someone changes the situation.

VERIFICATION TECHNIQUES

Here, and in Figure 2-1, are guidelines for broadly verifying information used in analysis within your own department:

• **Use information you developed yourself.** To be completely in control of your own analysis, you may limit source

Figure 2-1.   Verification techniques.

1. Use information you developed yourself.

2. When using outside information, qualify it in your reports.

3. Double-check the year-to-year information to ensure it is reported consistently.

4. Compare your information to other sources.

5. Review methods for reporting change from one period to another.

6. Be fair. Avoid selecting only that body of information that supports your own bias.

7. Represent the other point of view to add credibility to your report.

8. When results are interpretive, say so in your report.

information to that developed within the department. The occasions when you can reasonably do this will be rather limited. Using only your own data is practical when your analysis is limited to departmental factors.

Example: You prepare a report each month summarizing a number of on-going, long-term projects. The purpose is to anticipate scheduling problems and to enable management to take steps to stay on track. Because your department gathers information throughout the month that relates to the schedule, it is fairly easy to create the report without going to any outside sources.

However, when a scheduling problem does arise, you then need to consult with the project manager so that an explanation can be included in your report. So when there are exceptions, you do need to use external data to supplement your report.

• **When using outside information, qualify it in your reports.** If some of the information going into your analysis was supplied from outside sources, specify this in your report. The individual reading your report should be given sources for all information. That tells whether a bias is likely, and how dependable the sources might be.

Example: You are preparing a report for the vice president, who is thinking of hiring home-based workers. Demographics referenced in your report support the contention that home use of automation is on the rise. But what if the statistics were compiled by a company that manufactures microcomputers? How objective is your report?

• **Double-check the year-to-year information to ensure it is reported consistently.** Be sure to check carefully when more than one year's numbers are being used. Any changes in the method or timing of compilation will distort your analysis.

Example: You are tracking reported sales volume for a competing company. You are careful to look for any changes in reporting method, fiscal year, acquisitions or spinoffs—all factors that would distort the year-to-year analysis. In cases of such changes, the current and past year information needs adjustment so that all information in your analysis is reported on a like basis. Without this important step, the entire analysis will be wrong.

• **Compare your information to other sources.** Many forms of information are easily verified by checking with a second source. Also, the existence of a second source could eliminate unnecessary research for your analysis.

> *Example:* You are tracking the cost of overtime to support your request for a higher payroll budget. Your numbers can be checked with the actual payroll costs compiled and tracked in the payroll department. Doing so eliminates errors and, perhaps, adds to your analysis. The value of benefits and taxes withheld, added to your knowledge of the base hourly rate, makes your analysis more accurate.

• **Review methods for reporting change from one period to another.** Be extremely careful in developing any form of analysis involving reporting of changes in factors from one time period to another. There is a vast difference between reporting actual change and degree of change; some methods may distort the truth rather than represent it.

> *Example:* You are tracking the number of transactions generated in your department from one month to the next. The first month in your study is assumed to have an "index" value of 100. Each subsequent month is compared and reported to the index. That could be an appropriate method, assuming that the first month's value is truly representative. But what if that month's transactions were exceptionally high or exceptionally low? Unless you can establish an absolute representative starting point, percentage of change, indexing, and other similar methods may be troublesome for your analysis.

• **Be fair. Avoid selecting only that body of information that supports your own bias.** Because you are human, you are subject to human error. One form of error is to seek out information that supports the conclusion you have already drawn, or that you would like others to draw. You may do this unconsciously, even when struggling to remain as objective as possible. A good analyst will always remain open-minded to the possibility that basic assumptions are flawed. No one likes to admit this, especially if a number of hours have already been invested in preparing the analysis. But remember, it's better to catch the error *before* making a request based on flawed data, than to proceed knowing your claim is wrong.

• **Represent the other point of view to add credibility to your report.** A decision maker will be impressed by a comprehensive and well-researched report. The same decision-maker will be even more especially impressed when you go the extra step: playing devil's advocate and pointing out arguments *against* what you're recommending.

This is a powerful technique for strengthening your argument. By presenting arguments against your ideas *before* anyone else has the chance to do so, you defuse the point, show why and how it's flawed, and then direct attention back to the argument you really want to make: why your idea should be given approval.

> *Example:* You have prepared an analysis of photocopy machine use, as part of your recommendation that the company invest in another machine for your department. Your argument is based on the fact that several departments now share the same machine; that the machine is old and frequently down for repairs; and that the cost of idle time is higher than the cost of a new machine plus one year's maintenance. However, you include a second possible solution: to buy a machine for another department on the same floor, and give the older machine to your department. Your argument against this: Your department uses the machine to a higher degree than any other group on the same floor.

• **When results are interpretive, say so in your report.** Never let it be assumed that the numbers you present are absolute. If you're using estimates, disclose that fact in a way that there can be no mistake. And if the numbers were developed from other data in an interpretive form, say this clearly.

> *Example:* You are preparing a report to forecast probable marketing results for a new subsidiary. Included in your study are

comparisons between the projected markets and previous ventures. In your report, however, you specify several points: the
comparisons are made to previous ventures in different regions,
in a different economy, and with different products. You are
interpreting these previous experiences as "typical," but you
also disclose that it is only one possible interpretation. The
information is not completely reliable, but it's all you have.

The important thing is not to pin down with absolute
certainty what will happen; that is rarely possible. It is important, however, to make sure the reader of your report understands the potential variability of outcome by disclosing your
methods and explaining your interpretations.

ASSUMPTION TESTING

Verifying the accuracy of your information is an important first
step in preparing a dependable analysis. The second step is to
ensure that your assumptions are sound. An assumption is a
belief you hold about the information being used, the direction
a trend is headed, and how other factors will be influenced by
that trend.

Example: You are preparing a departmental budget for the new
year. To estimate office supply expenses, you study the past
three years' expense levels. You see a consistent relationship
between the number of employees in the department and the
amount spent on supplies. You assume that the relationship is
dependable and significant, and prepare the new budget based
on the estimated number of people working in the department.

In this example, you spotted a relationship: more employees resulted in higher office supply expenses. Is that logical?
To a degree, it does make sense; more people consume more
supplies, thus the relationship can be supported. However,
what about other factors? Can this one assumption be used to
accurately estimate the future budget?

That's what is meant by assumption testing. You start with one belief or observation (in this case the relationship between numbers of employees and office supply expenses) and then question the belief, looking for other factors. The test consists of critically reviewing the entire body of information being applied to the analysis. Ask yourself these questions:

- Should additional information be added?
- Is the information accurate?
- Does the information relate to the issue in a significant way?
- Could seemingly related historical outcomes be coincidental?

Let's apply these test questions to the example:

- **Should additional information be added?** The per-employee test appears dependable, based on consistent outcomes in the past. However, the study could be made more accurate by checking recent vendor prices changes as well.

- **Is the information accurate?** As long as your information was drawn from consistently and carefully kept records, there shouldn't be a problem. The departmental expenses could be verified by checking records in the accounting department, too.

- **Does the information relate to the issue in a significant way?** In other words, is there truly a relationship between the number of employees in a department and the level of office supply expense? How significant is the relationship? Enough to develop a trend you can use in the future? To determine this, check back to last year, and see how accurately the previous year's information could have been used to make a budget prediction.

- **Could seemingly related historical outcomes be coincidental?** It might seem unlikely, but it is possible. For example, what if the addition of new employees approximated inflationary trends in the office supply business?

Chapter 3

Narrowing the Odds

In this chapter I will scratch the surface of the world of statistics and probability and pull out a few useful and practical skills to help narrow the odds. The purpose of using statistics in analysis is to define the degree of dependability in your information. Being able to convey this to others helps define degrees of risk.

WORKING WITH AVERAGES

The first statistical technique to add to your arsenal is the mean, or average. An average is computed by adding up the values to be averaged, and then dividing the answer by the number of values involved.

Example: Over the last six months, your department processed the following number of transactions:

January	1,332
February	993
March	1,005
April	1,226
May	1,592
June	1,388
Total	7,536

To find the average, first add up the values. This has been done already, and the total is 7,536. The second step is to divide this total by the number of values in the set (in this case, six):

$$\frac{7,536}{6} = 1,256$$

The average transactions processed per month in the department was 1,256.

The formula for average is shown in Figure 3-1.

Example: You know you will be short-handed over the next six months, and you want to convince the budget committee of this fact—leading up to making a case to hire two additional employees. An analysis of the last six months of transaction levels does not reveal anything conclusive. How can the analysis be presented accurately and fairly, but showing a definite and dependable trend?

To answer this question we may employ a number of averaging techniques. These include the weighted average and the moving average.

WEIGHTED AVERAGES

A weighted average is one in which some values are given greater importance than others. Sometimes it is the more recent

Figure 3-1. Formula: average.

$$a = \frac{x_1 + x_2 + \ldots + x_n}{n}$$

a = average

x = value

n = number of values

values that are given extra weight, on the assumption that current information is more significant.

Weighting allows you to define and place that significance. The older the information becomes, the less reliable it is. You might need to include twelve months of figures, but you also know that the most recent months reflect what's really going on.

So how do you select one weighting method over another? (In the next few pages, some weighting techniques are explained.) You should select the method that is manageable, or not terribly difficult to compute, but that also gives you the most reliable information for your analysis. Depending on the circumstances, you might believe that only last month's figures are reliable; in some cases, you might assign equal weighting value to the last two or three months.

Generally speaking, the more quickly the situation changes, the more obsolete older information becomes. We show several weighting methods mainly to demonstrate the variety of ways the task can be completed. You should strive for the highest degree of accuracy in your weighting, on the basis of past reports and actual outcomes. For example, if your budgeting was very close when you used one particular form of weighting, that probably means it is the most reliable method to use. But if you were off by a degree, experiment with other weighting methods until you find one that works better for you.

There are any number of weighting methods; we will consider three, each of which can be calculated without extensive need for complicated math. All three will be applied to the same six-month period of the earlier examples.

Weighting Method 1

Under the first method, the most recent month is given twice the weighted value of the other months. This makes the latest month's value far more significant than any preceding month.

	Number	Weight	Value
January	1,332	1	1,332
February	993	1	993
March	1,005	1	1,005
April	1,226	1	1,226
May	1,592	1	1,592
June	1,388	2	2,776
Total		7	8,924

Notice that the set now contains seven values, not six.

$$\frac{8,924}{7} = 1,275$$

Weighting Method 2

The second method is a variation of the first. In this case, months in the older half of the set are given values of 1, and the more recent months are given higher values. For purpose of illustration, we will triple their value:

	Number	Weight	Value
January	1,332	1	1,332
February	993	1	993
March	1,005	1	1,005
April	1,226	3	3,678
May	1,592	3	4,776
June	1,388	3	4,164
Total		12	15,948

Now, with a total count of twelve values, the average is calculated as:

$$\frac{15,948}{12} = 1,329$$

Weighting Method 3

The third weighting method, called the sum-of-the-years digits, involves a bit more math. The oldest month in the set is assigned a value of 1 and the weighted value of each later month is increased by 1; so in a set of six, the most recent month will have a value of 6:

	Number	Weight	Value
January	1,332	1	1,332
February	993	2	1,986
March	1,005	3	3,015
April	1,226	4	4,904
May	1,592	5	7,960
June	1,388	6	8,328
Total		21	27,525

$$\frac{27,525}{21} = 1,311$$

This method produces a slightly lower average. It is also time-consuming and mathematically intense when dealing with an especially large set of numbers. Imagine the complexity of calculation with a set of 100 or more values.

THE MOVING AVERAGE

You might have noticed, in the previous examples, that the development of an average, by itself, is of only limited value. A solitary number is meaningless unless it is compared to something else. This is the case no matter what types of numbers are involved. Analysis depends on comparison. You know the average of the last six months, but you don't know whether the *trend* is increasing or decreasing. And that's usually what you need to know.

The best way to begin seeing the direction of a trend over time is with the moving average. With a moving average, a series of calculations is performed periodically (such as at the end of each month). The results can then be plotted, and a direction will emerge.

Example: Over the past six months, you have been tracking the number of transactions processed in your department. You want to anticipate high-volume periods and also to support a request for staff increases next year. You know that your only chance for approval will be to prove that the transaction trend is upward.

The following number of transactions were processed:

January	1,332
February	993
March	1,005
April	1,226
May	1,592
June	1,388
Total	7,536

To determine the six-month trend, use the moving average. First do a series of three-month simple averages:

1. *March:*

January	1,332
February	993
March	1,005
Total	3,330
Average	1,110

2. *April:*

February	993
March	1,005
April	1,226
Total	3,224
Average	1,075

3. *May:*

March	1,005
April	1,226
May	1,592
Total	3,823
Average	1,274

4. *June:*

April	1,226
May	1,592
June	1,388
Total	4,206
Average	1,402

To summarize, the series of three-month moving averages shows:

	Average
Jan.–Feb.–Mar.	1,110
Feb.–Mar.–Apr.	1,075
Mar.–Apr.–May	1,274
Apr.–May–June	1,402

Overall, the trend in this example is rising. The moving average is growing over time.

Of course, this might not necessarily be the final conclusion. There may be other factors to consider, such as seasonal variation, one-time increases in sales due to one big customer's special orders, or addition of a new line of business not included in previous outcomes. All these possibilities have to be taken into account if your interpretation of the analysis is to be accurate.

Moving averages may also be weighted. You might find it desirable to weight the latest month more heavily than the previous two, or to employ a simplified version of sum-of-the-years digits averaging.

In most cases, the three-month example is probably not a large enough selection to identify a definite trend. However, if the trend is followed over a longer period of time, and if a greater number of months is used in each average, a definite trend will emerge.

The difficulty is that a lot of math is involved. That means a greater chance of error, or at least much more time required to maintain the analysis. If you are dealing with a twelve-month average, for example, that requires computing the twelve values each month, finding the average, and then entering it into the analysis.

EXPONENTIAL MOVING AVERAGE

A short cut to the moving average is called the exponential method. Using the *exponential moving average* allows you to avoid a complex number of calculations, even when a large number of values are involved each month. It also adds a desirable degree of weighting to the calculation.

You can calculate exponential moving average using a worksheet like the one shown in Figure 3-2. To show how this is filled in, we will calculate the exponential moving average for the six months of transactions, using a three-month moving average as before.

The first step is to calculate the exponent. This is a value equal to 2 divided by the number of values in the set. In this case, three months will be used, so the exponent is:

$$\frac{2}{3} = .667$$

Enter the exponent on the worksheet in column 5. For the first period (January, February, and March), a simple average is calculated:

$$\frac{1,332 + 993 + 1,005}{3} = 1,110$$

Enter this into the worksheet in column 7. For the subsequent periods, use this procedure:

Step 1:   Enter the new month's value in column 2.
Step 2:   Enter the previous period's value from column 7, in column 3.

Figure 3-2. Worksheet for calculating exponential moving average.

(1) PERIOD	(2) VALUE	(3) PRIOR	(4) FACTOR	(5) EXP.	(6) NEW VALUE	(7) E.M.A.

Step 3:   Subtract the previous period's value (column 3) from the new month's value (column 2). Enter the result in column 4 as the current factor.

Step 4:   Multiply the value in column 4 by the exponent in column 5. Enter the result in column 6.

Step 5:   Add the new value in column 6 to the previous E.M.A. in column 7. If the value in column 6 is negative, subtract it from the prior E.M.A. Enter the new E.M.A. in column 7.

An example of the filled-in worksheet is shown in Figure 3-3.

Note that any negative values in column 6 are subtracted to form the new period's exponential moving average. In this example, there is only one negative value, in the June calculation. The exponential procedure can be carried forward for an indefinite number of new periods, and updated without the need for huge recalculations. It can be used with consistent weighting and accuracy, even when hundreds of values are included in the test.

DEGREES OF DEPENDABILITY

Averages—weighted, moving, or both—are useful but basic tools in the analyst's hands. They help you to make your point to the decision makers in your company, to reduce a long column of numbers to a meaningful graph or sentence, and to explain your conclusion clearly.

There may still be doubt, however, in the minds of the decision makers. They may ask, How dependable is your information?

The *degree* of dependability, in its most basic form, depends on the variation in range of the numbers under study. If the numbers, for the most part, are close to the average, then the analysis will be based on fairly consistent, dependable information. However, if the values fluctuate far above and

Figure 3-3. Worksheet for calculating exponential moving average (filled in).

(1) PERIOD	(2) VALUE	(3) PRIOR	(4) FACTOR	(5) EXP.	(6) NEW VALUE	(7) E.M.A.
March						1,110
April	1,226	1,110	116	.667	77	1,187
May	1,592	1,187	405	.667	270	1,457
June	1,388	1,457	− 69	.667	− 46	1,411

below the average, then any analysis you perform will be less dependable.

One method for reducing variation in the average is to simply drop off the highest and the lowest values. This is appropriate in many circumstances in business.

Example: You are preparing a study of the average sick time claimed in your department. Last year, the following days were claimed by employees:

Employee	Days
1	11
2	6
3	8
4	203
5	5
6	9
7	0
8	4
9	10

The two extremes are seen in employee number 4 (203 days) and employee number 7 (zero days). Let's first compute the average using all numbers. The total for all 9 employees is 256 days:

$$\frac{256}{9} = 28.4 \text{ days}$$

You know, just by your experience as a manager, that 28.4 days is not a fair average. But when the highest and lowest values are dropped from the field, leaving only seven people, the average changes. In this case, the total is 53:

$$\frac{53}{7} = 7.6 \text{ days}$$

With the two extremes eliminated, the calculated average is much closer to what you can truly expect in the future.

The degree of variance in a set of numbers is called the dispersion, or the spread. This is useful for placing a relative definition of variance, which improves your ability to communicate with decision makers and to support your analysis. Dispersion can be measured through calculation of *mean absolute deviation,* or the average of distances between the values and the average of the values. A worksheet for this calculation is shown in Figure 3-4.

> *Example:* Mean absolute deviation is a measurement of the square of distances between numbers and the average of those numbers. Using the six-month transaction example again, the calculation can be quickly shown on the worksheet (see Figure 3-5).

The next step is to divide the total of the squared values by the number of periods, or six:

$$\frac{269,166}{6} = 44,861$$

Figure 3-4. Worksheet for calculating mean absolute deviation.

PERIOD	NUMBER	AVERAGE	DISTANCE	SQUARE

Figure 3-5. Worksheet for calculating mean absolute deviation (filled in).

PERIOD	NUMBER	AVERAGE	DISTANCE	SQUARE
January	1,332	1,256	76	5,776
February	993	1,256	263	69,169
March	1,005	1,256	251	63,001
April	1,226	1,256	30	900
May	1,592	1,256	336	112,896
June	1,388	1,256	132	17,424
Total	7,536			269,166

This is the dispersion factor. By itself, the factor is not revealing. To get to the meaningful statistic concerning this range of numbers, there are two more steps. First, find the square root of the dispersion factor. A square root is the number which, when multiplied by itself, will equal your target number. The square root of 44,861 is 211.8 (rounded). This answer is called standard deviation.

The final step is actually identifying the degree of dependability as a percentage. To arrive at that, divide standard deviation by the average, or 1,256:

$$\frac{211.8}{1,256} = 16.9\%$$

Note that the answer is reported as a percentage. This is referred to in statistics as the coefficient of variation. This is the degree of variation, or relative dependability, in the set of six months of transactions. You may now accurately state to the decision makers that your averages and analysis are dependable within 16.9%. However, by itself, that information might not be of particular interest. This percentage really only becomes significant when you are able to compare it to a previous, similar calculation.

FAIRNESS IN SELECTING INFORMATION

Pinning down the accuracy of estimates or groupings of numbers used in analysis helps further determine whether or not you have been fair in selecting your raw data. It's often a series of trials that determine, once and for all, whether or not you have chosen information for your analysis accurately. Some guidelines for remaining fair in your selection of information are summarized below and in Figure 3-6:

• **Ask others for their opinions.** People in your department, fellow managers, and employees in the accounting department are potentially valuable sources of information. They may also be helpful in formulating the best approach to analysis. Don't try to develop your analysis in isolation. Ask for ideas, opinions, and help from other employees. And listen carefully; when you find good advice, take it.

• **Be sure you know where the information comes from.** Whenever you receive data from another department, make sure you know the source. Don't depend on its accuracy just because it's in writing. Remember, whenever you're dealing with a human being, human error is always lurking nearby. And even when the information comes from an automated system, human error is still a factor.

• **Check it yourself.** The thorough analyst is always willing to verify source data. That means asking the right questions, adding up a column again, going back to the source and seeing the numbers for yourself. Verify and then double check; then verify again if necessary.

• **Make sure that information you compare is, in fact,**

Figure 3-6. Guidelines: selecting information.

1. Ask others for their opinions.

2. Be sure you know where the information comes from.

3. Check it yourself.

4. Make sure that information you compare is, in fact, related.

5. Check back later to see how closely your analysis matched actual outcome.

6. When something doesn't work, change it.

7. Develop easy systems to capture valuable information you might need later.

8. Audit your own files.

related. It happens too often that information is so welcome that it's automatically worked into an analysis, even when it doesn't really belong. If you are comparing two different groups of information, first make sure they are truly related. Don't allow yourself to react to the event of getting information, without also ensuring that it's information you can use.

• **Check back later to see how closely your analysis matched actual outcome.** A good method for improving your track record as an analyst is to go back later, review your numbers, and see how they worked out. Where were you right and where did you go wrong? The answers will help you to sharpen your skills the next time around.

• **When something doesn't work, change it.** Don't make the mistake of failing to change something, even after learning it's wrong. There is no reason to stay with a plan in the name of tradition, consistency, or wishful thinking. Make changes, even if it means having no analysis. Let's face it, a lack of information is preferable to widely published wrong information.

• **Develop easy systems to capture valuable information you might need later.** Begin building an information bank in your own department. Keep records relating to the work of the department, the time equipment is broken down, hours spent in specific routines, error rates, transactions processed, and so forth. Any information you can imagine needing to make your point in the future is worth gathering today. A word of caution, however: The process of gathering your information bank should not be so time consuming that the cost of getting it exceeds its value.

• **Audit your own files.** Once you have an information bank, it is important to recognize that inaccurate information can find its way in. Check your files periodically. Go back over a random portion, looking for problems of accuracy and completeness. If you find a lot of problems, change procedures.

USING NUMBERS WITH CONFIDENCE

Forecasting is often entered into with misunderstandings, and resolved with compromise. But remember, no one really knows what will occur in the future; so a compromise makes as little sense as depending completely on a prediction in the first place. Two people, both operating unscientifically and without a sound basis, are extremely unlikely to compromise their positions in such a way that the solution will be the best possible one. You can change that. The secret is to recognize analysis for what it is, and to discuss the future not in terms of whether your numbers are right or wrong, but in terms of what they reveal. Here are some guidelines:

- **Remember, a forecast is only an estimate.** When trying to predict the future, it's very easy to lose sight of the purpose. Forecasts are meant to serve as a rule of thumb, a general guideline to indicate what *might* occur *if* a series of assumptions are true, *if* certain actions are taken, or *if* market conditions occur or are put into place. The goal is to spot the likelihood of outcome.

- **Analysis can support or destroy a belief; that is its value.** Many a budget meeting begins with a series of beliefs. All the people in the room stubbornly hold onto their own beliefs. Unfortunately, it's rare for any two people to agree. So the prediction problem is compounded. A logically prepared analysis can and does get through this problem, and allows you to make your point without all the ego-based problems often experienced in any future-based project.

- **It's all right to be wrong, as long as the prediction helped spot future risk. The real problems arise when someone wants to be right and ends up ignoring the risks altogether.** Your analysis and review will be wrong some of the time. That's not a problem as long as you were able to point out to the decision makers where potential problems and risks lay; and if, through that process, your company was able to avoid the risks in response to your efforts.

CONVERTING HUNCHES

Have you ever found yourself in the frustrating position of *knowing* you were right about something, but being unable to prove it? In your personal life, you may be free to appeal to other people to trust your hunch about something. In business, it's very unlikely you can get away with the same thing. Businesspeople want proof. This is one of the areas where accountants and others who take the analytical approach have a big advantage.

So when you know you're right, but you have no proof to make your point, what can you do to convert that hunch convincingly? Here are some ideas:

• **Seek the bottom line solution.** To repeat: No matter what the topic, begin your analysis with the idea that there is a bottom line involved. Every problem in business relates in some way to profit and loss. Find it, and you will also find the most appropriate method for developing your analysis. You will also make your point with the decision maker.

• **Find at least one tangible aspect and emphasize that.** You might conclude that there simply is nothing "bottom line" about a particular problem. But remember, all you need is one aspect. Emphasize that aspect, even if the improvement in the bottom line is extremely minor.

• **Begin your analysis by explaining that the topic is not easily converted to numbers.** When the subject being dis-cussed is not very tangible, start out by stating that point clearly. For example, you want to ask for new equipment in your department, knowing instinctively that it will more than pay for itself. You *know* that employees will use their time more efficiently, reduce idle time or errors, or work faster on more up-to-date equipment. However, you can't define these points in absolute terms, and even estimates are nothing more than best guesses. But remember that at these times, a best guess expressed in terms of the numbers is much more powerful than an opinion without documentation.

• **Assume the point of view that even a partial explanation is better than a pure hunch.** Hunches carry no weight on paper. They are at best opinions and may even appear to be emotional reactions rather than facts. Even if you come up with only one example of how your analysis proves the company will save money by approving your idea, that is better than having nothing at all to offer.

FINDING THE RIGHT DATA

A purely objective and scientific analysis begins with no prem-ise whatsoever. But in a corporate setting, there is almost always an agenda, hidden or otherwise. And people study facts and figures in search of support for their agenda. This is not dishonest; it's human. Few people who want to prove a point will choose data that disprove it—especially when supporting data are equally available. Accountants are just as likely to select the "right" facts to make their point as anyone else. And they are just as prone to error in the interpretation of facts and figures. They may see the immediate details that support one point while failing to grasp a larger and more important truth.

> *Example:* An accountant is preparing a monthly report comparing the sales forecast to actual sales. The latest results show that year-to-date actual sales have exceeded the forecast level. There is a positive variance.
>
> There is a different problem, however. While sales are rising, so are costs and expenses. The middle lines are growing at a faster rate than the top line. The inescapable conclusion: Net profits are being eroded.

As this example shows, it is quite easy for even a seasoned accountant to miss what's really taking place. If costs and expenses are growing at a faster pace than sales volume, there is no way for profits to increase at the same time. That's a mathematical impossibility. Yet, many managers will review budgets and forecasts and ignore the figures before their eyes.

Analysis cannot be limited to discovery of facts that support your point. In order to be useful and relevant, you will need to examine information more carefully. A key point:

To become a truly effective analyst, you need to look beyond the obvious. You need to see the truth.

Chapter 4

Reporting With Trends

From analysis, trends are developed. And the trend, properly used, presented, and explained, is the only road the corporate decision maker truly recognizes and knows how to travel.

USING RATIOS

Historical information by itself won't tell you for certain what to expect in the future. However, a consistent trend is a very compelling piece of evidence pointing to the likelihood of a specific future outcome.

However, you must sometimes deal with a complex array of financial information, endless columns and rows of related dollar values, unit counts, percentages, and fractions. How do you convert all that data into a simple and clear statement about what conclusions should be reached from your work?

The answer is found in the ratio, which is an abbreviated expression of two or more larger numbers—a form of financial shorthand. The ratio is expressed in one of three forms: as a percentage, as a factor or count, or as a relational expression (such as 2 to 1). Here are some key points to remember about ratios:

• **Any solitary number is meaningless.** The numbers are significant only in their comparison to other numbers. Sales or profits for the current year are meaningful only when compared to the same outcomes from previous years, or when expressed in some other form that has meaning to others, such as a profit expressed as a percentage of sales. On the departmental level, numbers defining error rates, productivity, and the volume of work processed, are significant only when compared as part of a trend. Without the comparison, the information is useless.

• **Be careful when comparing to a standard.** Comparing a number against an accepted standard is a common form of comparison. The danger is that the standard might not be fairly applied in every case. You often need to look beyond what the numbers indicate. You might discover that the truth is opposite what the number seems to indicate.

Example: A company has set a standard defect rate of 3 percent or lower; one production shift consistently sees errors above 5 percent. Does that mean that one shift has poor management? What if that shift is where all new employees are trained? Should the 3 percent standard then be applied? Probably not.

A key point to remember:

If you're really interested in the complete truth, always be willing to look beyond the numbers.

• **The ratio takes on meaning only when it is compared to the previous ratio using the same data.** Year-to-year comparisons are the basic method for trend reporting, at least in the accounting department. Quarterly, monthly, even weekly analysis is also common. The frequency period for your analysis should depend on the nature of the information. For example, you might decide to perform a month-to-month analysis of transactions processed if your processing occurs on a monthly cycle.

• **The two parts of the ratio must be related to one another.** It might seem obvious that the two sides of a ratio analysis must be related. However, many reports have been prepared *without* the required relationship.

An example of lack of relationship: What is the point in comparing the number of transactions processed in an insurance claims department to the changes in outstanding accounts receivable? There is no relationship between these two data sets. Sometimes the relationship is not obvious at first. If your department's work load changes with sales levels, comparing your error rate to sales volume may be appropriate. If you are proposing a change, such as hiring temporary help, changing operating procedures, purchasing upgraded equipment, or installing a more efficient internal system, you could use ratio analysis to prove the point that the error rate follows the trend in sales.

RATIOS IN NONFINANCIAL STUDIES

Ratios are usually associated with financial and accounting routines: budgeting, internal auditing, and other number-intensive activities. However, the techniques of developing ratios to express a larger grouping of numbers can be applied in any situation.

> *Example:* Your department's work involves a lot of computer terminal time. You have noticed signs of stress among employees, and are studying error rates to test your theory. You use ratios to compare the error rate to time an employee spends inputting.

> *Example:* The number of transactions processed by your department has been rising over the past two years; however, there has been no increase in staff. You express these facts in a brief report using ratios, to make your case for a budget increase.

> *Example:* Employees in your department use a photocopy machine two floors up. You study idle time and prepare a report with ratio summaries, to show that purchase of a new machine just for your department would be cost effective.

It is much easier to see a trend when ratios are used, for the reasons listed below and summarized in Figure 4-1:

• **Relationships between numbers are difficult to see and comprehend.** When you look at one set of numbers that change over a period of time, it is very difficult to visualize the significance of the change. When you add a second series of numbers *and* expect to comprehend the significance of how each set relates to the other, the problem is compounded. The relationship is terribly obscure.

The solution is to eliminate the use of long columns and rows of numbers in business reports. If they are needed at all, they should be included as appendix material. In the report itself, the relationships between numbers should be shown only in the form of ratios. Decision makers want simplified,

Figure 4-1. Advantages of ratios.

1. Relationships between numbers are difficult to see and comprehend.

2. Trends are impossible to spot in a column of numbers.

3. An excessively numerical report is hard to follow and far from interesting.

4. The numbers are not as interesting as the trend.

5. The limited space in a report is best used to interpret numbers and offer solutions.

accurate, timely, and concise summaries, with your ideas expressed clearly and in a way that is easily understood.

• **Trends are impossible to spot in a column of numbers.** Some people think analysis consists of listing a column of numbers and expecting those numbers to speak for themselves. If you offer a listing of numbers as your version of analysis, you miss a great opportunity.

Avoid passively giving numbers to other people. They can easily accumulate numbers on their own. Rather, take the opportunity to offer concrete advice, make recommendations to management, and propose changes that improve the bottom line. Take a chance. Shun the commonplace, passive numerical summary and replace it with strong ideas, supported with words instead of numbers, and backed up with ratios instead of lists.

• **An excessively numerical report is hard to follow and far from interesting.** Some people never learn the truth: that numbers are simply not very interesting. An accountant undoubtedly knows far more than what the numbers reveal. Decision makers would probably prefer to hear what the accountant *thinks* rather than see what he or she can prove. To avoid this trap and keep financial information in perspective, adopt this golden rule: Never prepare a report containing more numbers than words.

• **The numbers are not as interesting as the trend.** One common trap is becoming preoccupied with the numbers side of the job. Falling in love with the numbers is dangerous, because then you lose sight of the real human issues behind them. You must get away from the need to express issues in terms of math—debits and credits, columns and rows, profit and loss. All these technical details are there, to be sure. But what it's really all about is not numbers, but movement of issues, people, events. The numbers convey the essence of issues, but are not themselves the issue.

• **The limited space in a report is best used to interpret numbers and offer solutions.** Let's assume you are giving an oral presentation to the executive committee this afternoon.

You will be allowed to speak for two minutes. In that brief amount of time, what will you say? Or suppose you are asked for a written report that can run no longer than three pages. What information is compelling enough to include, and what should be left out?

In either case, you only take up time and space by putting too many numbers in your report. Use the time and space more productively and in a more interesting manner, by recommending positive changes. Use the numbers, expressed as ratios whenever possible, to prove your point and back up your claims. But emphasize the issues, advise management, and show the way to a solution.

Chapter 5

Developing the Trend

At what point does the analysis become interesting? When are you able to translate the merely statistical into a series of useful, meaningful, and significant forms of information?

A trend is a direction or movement that is under way. It is a series of events or figures that are related to one another, that can be studied to anticipate the future. Every financial and nonfinancial ratio becomes significant *only* when it is reviewed as the last entry in the trend. So a trend may also be thought of as the immediate history of facts and figures, the meat of the analysis, and the most accurate way to estimate and predict the future.

A trend, derived from analysis and proved by testing, is a verification of approach and technique. However, it is not yet interesting. It remains two-dimensional, lying flat on the table. The third dimension comes when the trend is developed— meaning that it is interpreted and its meaning explained. Then the trend gains depth.

When a trend is developed, it becomes more than a summary of information. To the decision maker reviewing it, the trend takes on life and color and represents the realities residing underneath the numbers.

What makes your analysis meaningful? When you are able to clearly point to the outcome as part of a trend over time, you will also be able to report whether the current trend is positive or negative. Trends invariably show up as significant not for one or two isolated periods, but over a longer term, such as six to twelve months or more. The longer-term trend will show a clear direction that you can take to the table and report with confidence.

Any movement or change in a trend, including the *lack* of change, is significant in some way. It might mean that controls put into place two months ago are working; it might prove that positive (or negative) forces are still at work; it might even prove that the trend itself cannot be dependably studied.

TYPES OF TRENDS

It would be very simple if trends always moved in the same direction and at the same rate. But they don't. The truly interesting part of the management task is contending with the unknown, making decisions without enough hard information, and learning from past experience. That's where your analytical skills are really put to the test.

In doing your job, you have already dealt with trend interpretation, although you might not have given it that name. You will recognize them, though, when you become aware of the six categories of trends.

Category 1: Up

Everyone's favorite trend is the "up" trend. By its name, the up trend implies a positive change—sales, profits, new orders, or some other prosperous outcome. When the factor is negative and on the increase, it should be reported as a "down" trend, if only to avoid confusion. For example, when a negative variance is increasing from month to month, that's not an "up" trend at all.

Up trends tend to slow down over time. Nothing continues to rise forever. In projecting the future of any trend, it is wise to calculate a gradual decline in the *rate* of growth, even if the up trend continues.

Example: During its first year in business, a new company's sales doubled in each quarter. The owner enthusiastically pointed to this trend as a positive sign. However, the accountant quite correctly pointed out that it was too soon to call the change a trend and that even if the positive direction were to continue indefinitely, it would be unrealistic to expect 100% increases in every quarter.

Category 2: Down

A down trend is invariably negative. But identifying such a trend should not be considered bad news in and of itself. The point in performing any analysis is to spot trouble before it's too late. When you discover a "down" trend, the important thing is to take immediate action to slow it down, stop it, and reverse it. Don't waste time trying to assign blame; focus on fixing the negative trend. Remember:

> Any analysis is worthwhile only if management is able to act on information discovered as a result.

Down trends may be represented by declining sales or profits, or a lower than expected volume of orders; or by *increasing* costs and expenses, errors or defects, and other factors affecting profits, efficiency, productivity, and other measurements of results.

Category 3: Stable

A stable or unmoving trend can be either reassuring or the most difficult to interpret. It is reassuring if nonmovement is desirable. It will be difficult to interpret if you don't know what the lack of movement indicates; it could mean there is no useful trend to interpret.

Of course, any trend analysis should begin with the premise that you know what a "good" outcome is; otherwise, you simply don't know what to look for. If maintaining a relationship between two sets of data is a positive trend, then a stable result is desirable. This is often seen when tracking percentage relationships—direct costs or profits as a percentage of sales, for example. Maintaining an acceptable level is the desired result:

Example: The accounting department reports on a number of financial ratios, including the relationship between current assets and current liabilities (known as the current ratio). The desirable level is 2 to 1 (two dollars in assets for every dollar in liabilities). If the ratio falls below this level, it indicates poor planning of working capital; if it goes above, it implies poor use of available funds. As long as the current ratio remains fairly stable at about 2 to 1, that's a positive sign.

In some cases, you're looking for a change, so a stable trend is the same as no news. You can't tell whether the changes you instituted are working, or whether the problem is getting worse. In such cases, a different test may be needed.

Category 4: Random

We undertake analysis on the assumption that some valuable information will come from it: good news, bad news, or confirmation or denial of a premise. But we also have to face a reality: Some information does not conform to the usual trending norms.

A truly random set of information is one that cannot be predicted with trend analysis. The outcome of a particular study may, in fact, be beyond your ability to analyze, and must be assumed to be completely random.

Example: You have been trying to analyze the trend in employee sick leave in your department. You know the average, based on a study of past years, and you know what is reasonable. But you finally conclude that there is no way to accurately predict when you will be shorthanded. You can estimate the total sick days over the period of a year. But the incidence from week to week is a random event.

If your attempts at analysis do not prove anything, you might be faced with a random outcome or, more accurately, a set of information that cannot be trended out. Many types of financial outcomes are reactive. They change based on movement in other data. So rather than developing in some predictable way, the trend evolves based on the influence of outside forces. The outcome of a particular study may, in fact, be beyond your ability to analyze, and must be assumed to be completely random.

Category 5: Changing

Analysts often make the mistake of looking so intently at the past that they miss a change in the current data. Remember, nothing goes up (or down) forever. Trends change direction.

Trends may change because you took action in the recent past—to reverse a negative direction, for example. Or you might have acted to encourage and support a positive trend, but it changed anyway. Trends may also change because of the influence of outside factors—everything from inflation and interest rates to a change in management policy, actions of the competition, or the consumer's perception of prices and values.

> *Example:* Your department has been processing a consistent number of transactions per employee for the last three years. In fact, there has been a slight improvement in overall productivity per person. Now, though, the trend has suddenly reversed itself. The number of transactions per employee has suddenly fallen. To find out the underlying cause, you will need to investigate further. The important point here, though, is that you *know* from the analysis that there has been a change in the trend's direction.

Category 6: New

The last type is not a trend at all, at least not yet. An emerging trend cannot be given value for many periods, perhaps for years. The only time new information can be analyzed is in relation to some well-understood and generally accepted outside standard. The current ratio, comparing current assets to current liabilities, is one example of this. It is universally understood that this ratio should be 2 to 1 or higher. You do not need a long history of outcomes; even for a brand-new company, you can compare information to the overall standard. This will not be the case for every type of information.

Example: The manager of a new division reports profits of 9% of sales for the first year and a forecast of 14% for the second year—significantly higher than companywide profits. When questioned about this forecast, the manager reports that the one-year trend was simply continued into the second year. Other division managers knew that a 14% profit was unreasonable.

In such a situation, there are several forecasting choices that would be more realistic than simply continuing a trend established in a short period.

1. *Comparison to other divisions during their first two years of operation.* The manager could have compared the divisional history to similar periods of other divisions. As long as the information involves the same company, even a substantial time gap produces relatively dependable information. The *trend* is the important thing, not necessarily the number or percentages involved.
2. *Application of an industry standard, if available.* It might be that in a particular industry, "normal" annual profit can be identified from the public record.
3. *A reduction in the curve of the trend.* If the manager truly believes the upward trend will continue (even without proof), reducing the curve will make it more acceptable to experienced decision makers, who will recognize that first-year trends are not trends at all.

EXPRESSING RATIOS IN THE TREND

Identify the starting point: learning how to state the trend in the shorthand expression of the ratio. However, it is not enough to reduce the numbers to ratios and then just report them. You could group the ratios, which is easier to follow. But it's almost as uninteresting as the original numbers would be. To make your numbers come to life, you must add some explanation.

There are a number of ways to express the ratios so that your audience will appreciate their significance. These are summarized in Figure 5-1 and listed below:

• **Use averages to smooth out results.** In a trend, the month-to-month numbers, without the benefit of averaging, will appear to be erratic, opposite of the general direction of the trend, or otherwise misleading.

The longer the period being averaged, the greater the effects of smoothing. In the stock market, for instance, a 200-day moving average is used. This high level of detail is easily managed by computer but, in other business applications, would prove a mathematical burden with only limited benefits.

Figure 5-1. Ways to express ratios.

1. Use averages to smooth out results.

2. Report with indexing, but cautiously.

3. Percentage change is a popular method.

4. Measurement against an external standard could be the most significant.

5. Internal standards might be needed, too.

In most applications you will encounter, a more simplified version of averaging will suffice.

• **Report with indexing, but cautiously.** Reporting with the use of an index is appealing to many, but proceed with great caution. An index is a stationary, accepted standard against which a number of other figures are compared. The stationary value is given the value of "1" (or, 100 percent). Then, other figures are relatively higher or lower than the index.

You may assign a "standard" to a series of numbers or relationships, and then index changes from that standard. For example, you might determine that the typical number of transactions run through your department in one month is 2,000. As the numbers change, they are indexed on the assumption that 2,000 has a value of 1 (or 100 percent). So any number less than that will be lower than 1 (.98, for example); and any number of transactions higher than the agreed-upon norm would be greater (1.02, for example).

Indexing makes a lot of sense in several applications, and is one of the easiest methods of reporting trends. For example, you might decide that each subsidiary in a company should earn a net profit of 8 percent per year. That becomes the index, and all results are then measured against it. Or, your department might be able to process the average report in forty-six hours. You assign that number of hours as the index value, and then judge each subsequent report by how much more or less time it takes.

However, what if your index norm is not typical? For example, what if 2,000 transactions was not the most representative number in the first example above? Even with the most careful and diligent study, you can err using indexing. Be careful in assigning index values. Make sure the "norm" you select is fair, and also that it remains fair in the future.

• **Percentage change is a popular method.** One of the most widely used methods, and one that often gives you a reasonable trend indicator, is reporting with percentage of change from one period to the next. The percentage change is well accepted and easily understood. For example, you might report in a meeting that "the department processed 5,000 orders, versus 2,500 the month before." But the impact is much greater if you report that "this month's processing volume was 100 percent higher than the month before."

The danger in percentage reporting is that the expression of a trend can easily become distorted. If last month's outcome was untypical, then the percentage of change this month is distorted accordingly. And some forms of information do not lend themselves well to percentage-of-change reporting. Suppose, for example, that you are comparing the numbers of employees in the department and the number of transactions processed. Your goal is to find an efficient relationship and then to spot trends that move below it. In this example, a percentage-of-change report will be of no value. What you need is to ensure that the relationship between two sets of data remains relevant from one period to another.

• **Measurement against an external standard could be the most significant.** Some information has the greatest significance when it's compared to a generally accepted standard, rather than to previously reported information. For example, in your industry, the typical production shift is expected to experience 2 percent defects; this is a generally accepted external standard. One shift in your company consistently reports defects of 5 percent or more—much higher than the industry norm. While there may be reasons for this, the indication at first is that there could be a problem.

• **Internal standards might be needed, too.** You might need to operate under a standard imposed from within. For example, senior management might set a performance standard, a profit goal, or a sales quota.

For example, the sales manager in your division expects every salesperson to generate a specific level of gross sales in a given month. He insists that when someone's output is lower than that level, it's because the salesperson is not making enough calls. Historical information bears out this belief. Thus, the standard for the sales division is that every salesperson is expected to make a specified number of sales calls per month.

MEDIAN AND MODE

In many cases, you will not be interested in the average value as much as you will be in the *typical* value. There is a big difference. The average is a calculation of the middle range value in a distribution of values. As part of a larger trend, the average is the calculation of choice in most cases. You might achieve more accuracy by calculating one of two other values: median or mode.

Median

Let's continue with the earlier example of average employee sick days. Because one employee was out a great deal (203 days), the straight average for all nine employees was 28.4 days. When the two extremes are eliminated, the seven remaining employees average out to 7.6 days. This is far more accurate. Obviously, you would expect the "typical" employee to report in sick about 7 or 8 days per year, and not 28 days.

Recognizing that high and low values are untypical is not always easy, however. So as an alternative, you can calculate the median, which is nothing more than the value in the middle of the distribution. Start with the list of nine employees:

Employee	Days
1	11
2	6
3	8
4	203
5	5
6	9
7	0
8	4
9	10

Next arrange the list in either ascending or descending order (it doesn't matter which, since you want only to find the *middle* value):

203
11
10
9
8
6
5
4
0

In this distribution, 8 is the median. It is the value in the very middle of the list. In an even-numbered list, the median would be two values; to reduce it to one number, you would average the two middle values.

You could use the median to estimate the "typical" employee sick leave days per year, and it would be about as accurate as the modified average—in this case, at least. Even that is no guarantee that the use of median over average is always fair. The key is to have knowledge about your information, and to apply it intelligently.

For example, as a manager, you already know what a reasonable (or typical) number of days would be for the study. This raises the question: Why perform the exercise if you already know? The answer is, because in presenting information for others, you will need to establish the basis. You need to avoid going into a meeting and claiming information without being able to back it up with hard proof.

You know, as a manager, that the unmodified average in this case was far overstated, so that some alternative method was needed. Both elimination of high and low values, and median, produced a more reasonable outcome.

Mode

Another calculation worth knowing is the mode—the value that appears more than once. It is most useful to find the typical characteristics of a distribution, rather than the average.

Example: You are analyzing sales for a mail order company that sells only two items. Your goal: to estimate typical sales in the future. Your listing from last month contains 45 sales of $39.95 each and one sale of $352. So $39.95 is the mode, because it appears more than once.

In this simplified example, mode is more accurate as a measurement of typical sales in the future; using an average would be misleading and inaccurate.

Mode can be used only in isolated cases, however. Some potential problems:

1. *There might be no mode at all.* In the list of nine employees in the previous case, there is no mode—because no one value appears more than once. So even if you wanted to figure the mode, it isn't there.
2. *Mode isn't always revealing.* A value could appear more than once, but still be untypical. For example, what if two employees had each been absent last year for zero days? The mode of the distribution would be zero, while you would reasonably expect absenteeism to be greater.
3. *A list could have two or more modes.* If more than one value appears on the list more than once, then you have more than one mode. You could have three, four, five, or more modes to a rather limited list, meaning the mode is not as useful as you'd like.

Chapter 6

What the Trend Reveals

In most instances, trend outcomes are apparent to everyone. A positive or a negative outcome is obvious, and there is no big secret to solving the analysis puzzle. However, when reporting a newly developed trend for the first time, be aware that what might seem obvious might need careful study and reconsideration. An honest and comprehensive evaluation might lead you to conclude the exact opposite of what you thought at first.

INTERPRETING THE NUMBERS

It would seem that translating numbers to ratios, and then expressing those ratios as part of a trend, is a fairly straightforward process. However, the truth is not always so simple. Remember the precautionary points listed below and summarized in Figure 6-1:

• **The numbers must be consistent from one period to another.** One common flaw in analysis is that banks of data become increasingly undependable from one period to another. This occurs because information is gathered inconsistently. When this happens, the trend is unavoidably inaccurate. The problem can come about in a number of ways. Most obvious is simply gathering different information from one

Figure 6-1. Key points: interpreting the numbers.

1. The numbers must be consistent from one period to another.

2. Any extraordinary items should be removed from current and past data.

3. New information could make previous data invalid after the fact.

4. Outside influence could distort an otherwise dependable trend.

5. Your interpretations might be accurate, but other versions could apply as well.

6. The absolute answer is rare.

period to another. Other mistakes happen because information is stored differently from one period to the next. An improvement in filing systems, coding, storage and retrieval, or organization of the company itself, all can mean that getting the same information in two consecutive years becomes difficult. It doesn't have to be a major change; even a simple event can create the problem.

• **Any extraordinary items should be removed from current and past data.** Accountants know only too well how results can be distorted by an extraordinary item—changes in inventory valuation, profit adjustments resulting from foreign exchange rates, and any number of other one-time profits or losses. On the departmental basis, any circumstance that distorts what is reported in your trend should be removed from the study. And make sure that in future periods, the adjusted basis is used for historical comparisons. The extraordinary items from past years should be removed and careful records kept on an as-adjusted basis.

Example: This year's transaction load includes several hundred processes repeated twice during a computer conversion. It would be inaccurate to count all of them as separate transactions.

• **New information could make previous data invalid after the fact.** You might have a completely valid file of information from the past several years, but because of changes this year those results have now become invalid. We cannot afford to assume that "valid" is a permanent state of affairs. When you think about it, changes on many levels affect the validity of a file of information, an assumption, or even a corporate belief.

Example: Part of your trend analysis is based on inventory of raw materials. This year, the valuation of inventory is changed. For historical information to remain valid, its value must be re-stated—a formidable task. You might have to begin your trend analysis from ground zero.

• **Outside influences could distort an otherwise dependable trend.** Internal changes are not the only factors that could distort your historical file. In some cases, an outside adjustment could have the same effect. For example, as part of a tax audit, income statements going back several years have to be modified. When outside influences change your historical file, you will need to incorporate the modification in your trend analysis.

• **Your interpretation might be accurate, but other versions could apply as well.** One thing to remember about reporting trends: Your conclusion is only one possible interpretation. Every trend interpretation is only an opinion.

Example: You present your analysis of growth in customer orders. From your data, you conclude that more customers are going to order from you in the future. A manager from the marketing department disagrees. He believes that the same number of customers will place orders, but that the average size of the order will grow. You both agree on the forecast increase in volume. You disagree as to the underlying causes.

• **The absolute answer is rare.** This is especially true when you are using historical information to make recommendations about the future. In the business world people constantly estimate and forecast the future, but rarely will they be able to pin down facts in absolute terms.

VERIFYING SOLUTIONS

Interpreting the trend is the heart of analysis—and the true challenge. What, indeed, does the result mean?

A series of broad assumptions, especially among those with an accounting background, prevent us from gaining the most from analysis. Be aware of these assumptions:

• **The "numbers" reveal fairly simple truths.** Accountants are accustomed to drawing up financial statements in a uniform and widely accepted format, interpreting the numbers based on widely known and believed standards, and reporting these results passively, without much comment. Thus, the belief goes, numbers are easy to interpret and read.

The truth is far different. In fact, people may read the numbers in a wide variety of ways. Interpretation will depend largely on your point of view, understanding of the issues underneath the numbers, and depth of knowledge about the company beyond your own sphere of influence. Just as problems are difficult to define to everyone's satisfaction, the meaning of an outcome is subject to endless debate.

• **There is only one right answer.** This is a dangerous assumption. There can be a number of right answers, or shades of right and wrong to an answer. The problem is, what's right from one point of view is wrong from another. Be aware that people have widely different agendas and, as a result, points of view.

• **Everyone has a similar agenda.** Not everyone who goes into a meeting wants the same thing. And not everyone who sees your analysis will agree with the interpretation you offer. You need to understand how other people's agendas are unique, and why. It does not make them wrong; it does mean that they confront a different set of problems each day than you do. So a different set of solutions is in order.

Avoid presenting your interpretation of a trend in absolute terms. "This indicates . . ." is more tactful than "This establishes beyond any doubt. . . ." You will know your solution is the best possible one when others admit you have identified a problem and a solution. Even though it might not help them, a successful outcome is difficult to ignore and impossible to dispute.

TESTING THE TREND

You also need to know how to test a trend. Is it still valid (or, was it valid to begin with), and what proof does it offer? Does that proof indicate anything of value to you and your fellow managers, executives, or employees? These are all valid questions that should be applied continuously to all trend reports and routines. Use these techniques to test your trend:

• **Test by purpose.** Begin your test by identifying the purpose. Is the analysis performed as part of a maintenance function, or to monitor a trend?

• **Revise by averaging method.** Many methods are reported on one of several averaging methods. Compare the outcome of your trend analysis by different methods. For example, try weighting rather than a simple moving average. How does the variation affect outcome? Is it more accurate, and why? Does the revised information point out directions of the trend more rapidly? Is the revised method easier to execute each month?

• **Consider modifying the information base.** Is the information you're using the most accurate, or would some modification of the data base be appropriate? In some cases, you begin a trend analysis based on what you have at hand, only to discover a better source later. If you change midstream, it will be necessary to go back and revise older trend reports.

• **Validate information continuously.** Never assume that one procedure will be valid indefinitely. Constantly question the validity of your procedures, information, and interpretation. The truly professional analyst is never satisfied with past successes, but is constantly looking for ways to improve the quality of information in the future. Analysis is an ongoing procedure; the methods employed to develop trends should be ever-changing as well.

Chapter 7

Budgeting With an Assumption Base

It would be unreasonable to expect people to spend weeks preparing a document that will never be looked at. If you are a leader of your company, you certainly would not want to waste employee time and effort in a meaningless exercise. If you are a department manager, there is certainly more pressing work to be done. We all want to believe that the work we perform has value.

But as unreasonable as it is to ask others and ourselves to waste time, often that's what budgeting is all about. We stay late every night for weeks and place similar demands on subordinates. We rush to meet deadlines, only to discover that the whole thing is being revised. We make up numbers without any logical reason, and they are accepted without question.

These are the reasons budgeting causes such dread. Everyone knows the budget is a useless waste of time when it is prepared under the usual method. You can change this, however, by suggesting to your management that the budgeting philosophy be changed—that it can be used as a profit center rather than as a waste of time.

Your company is constantly looking out for new ways to improve the bottom line. Yet few people realize that the budgeting process itself can be used as a profit center.

The usual process looks like this: weeks of discussion, filling out forms, more discussion, more forms, and, way beyond deadline, a "final" budget. Of course, that final version is changed yet again, so it's nearly the end of the first quarter before the budget is accepted. In some companies, the budget for the new year is barely finalized when six-month revision work starts.

In all this activity, there is little if any followup on the budget. Once the budget is done, no one looks at it again. There are no meetings to discuss variances and their causes. Or maybe causes are discussed, but no one takes any steps to fix the problem. So it goes on, until the next revision deadline or year-end.

What is wrong with this description? It is *not* budgeting! It's only filling out forms and passively finding and acknowledging problems. Lacking are the controls and actions that bring budgets to life, the followup, the investigation, and the reversal of discovered negative trends. Without these steps, the budgeting process has only gone a fraction of the way toward achieving its intended purpose.

The Purpose of the Budget

Let's start by exploring the purpose of the budget. It might seem that this is obvious, but ask a few co-workers, and you will soon have an interesting debate on your hands. In defining the budgeting process, keep these facts in mind:

• **Budgets are not absolute.** Many people, when they realize this point, will feel tremendous pressure removed from them. We can easily fall into the belief system that tells us our budgets must be accurate, or they have failed. This pressure leads to a silent conspiracy revolving around the budget, on all levels. Top management won't challenge obviously flawed procedures, if middle managers won't demand more from the process. Only by recognizing the truth about budgets can the problem be eased. You are *not* asked to accurately predict the future, only to identify the probabilities.

• **Most people are not good at guessing the future.** You might think that you are not a successful budget preparer because your budget was way off. But remember, very few people can guess the future accurately. Your success and confidence as a budget preparer will improve when you begin developing budgets using applicable assumptions. Everyone is in the same situation—afraid to get too specific, to prepare budgets without that little cushion. All this betrays the intended purpose of budgeting, and actually is contrary to the purpose the exercise is meant to provide.

• **You gain no points for accurate guesses.** A lot of importance is placed on the idea of accuracy in prediction, especially in those late weeks of the fiscal year when everyone is staying late working on the budget. But in fact, there is no real value in being the most accurate, or in coming closest to actual outcome. You will gain many more points by preparing the most useful and practical budgets. Why? Because only with such budgets will you be able to *affect* the future, to increase profits through control of expenses. Budgeting helps you to create a profit center by middle-line control, rather than by increasing sales or gross margins.

• **The real value of budgeting comes out in the form of variances.** It would surprise a lot of people to learn that, contrary to popular belief, variances are what give budgets value. It's not the *lack* of variances to report (as is commonly believed) that makes a budget worthwhile. It's uncovering an important variance that is worth tracking down and investigating. This assumes, of course, that someone does follow through. Unfortunately, the budgeting process doesn't usually go that far.

This is the key point. There is no value to the budgeting process if you do not follow through and take action, based on what you discover. This is true in all forms of analysis. You collect your numbers, think about what information they reveal, and then come to some conclusion. Then, however, you need to take action—to reverse negative trends, or to encourage and support positive trends.

So, in defining the purpose of budgeting, remember these key points:

- Budgets indicate problems or the unexpected. They can be used to focus on areas where more control is needed.
- Variances are forms of valuable information. Fast action leads to higher profits.
- Budgets are not absolute. They are standards we set for ourselves that we would like to meet. When actual outcome varies away from the standard, the budget tells us—but only if we ask. That question comes out when we perform the review.

A NEW APPROACH

I propose a new approach to budgeting, one that makes use of analysis to give the entire process real significance, and enables you to explain *why* the future comes out the way it does. With the more traditional passive approach to budgeting, this is impossible. The new approach is based on the simple idea that all budgets should be based on detailed, specific assumptions that make sense for each category of income, cost, or expense. Then, when the actual results come in, you can compare the assumption to the reality. The result: information that can be put to use to truly control future income and expenses.

Do you recognize this procedure? The office supplies portion of the departmental budget was developed by taking the previous year's actual expense and increasing that by 5 percent. The new number was then divided by 12 to arrive at each month's budget. This is the most commonly used method for developing a budget. But when you think about it, how do you explain an unfavorable variance? Perhaps a more important question is: Are you ever asked to explain the variances you experience? If you cannot explain variances in your own budget, then of what value is budgeting? And if company leaders don't demand an explanation, then they aren't doing their job either. In both cases, the budgeting process has failed.

Consider, though, how much more valuable that budget will be if it is built on a number of reasonable assumptions. Then, when variances do occur, they can be identified. Why go to the trouble of identifying the causes of unfavorable variances? Because then you can take corrective action.

> *Example:* Your department's current budget includes an allowance for office supplies. That budget was developed with a number of assumptions. Annual bulk purchases were scheduled in. Suppliers were contacted for current price levels. And an analysis showed that supply expenses rose when the number of employees in the department was increased. You plan to add two employees this year, so your office supply budget was coordinated with the timing of staff increases.

Here, a budget was developed based on factors that seem to have an effect on outcome. Bulk purchases (based on past patterns), pricing changes, and usage are all combined in a series of assumptions. When actual results occur, they can be compared to these assumptions.

THE PROCESS

The budgeting process is not just filling out blank worksheets, with columns for every month and rows for each expense classification. That's only the beginning, the very first step in a more comprehensive operating system. In fact, the visible budget worksheet is only the first of three major steps in the complete budget.

The second step is the monthly review. The budget becomes worthwhile only when the managers of each department sit down together and review the budget in the light of what actually happened in all the revenue, cost, and expense categories. In this review, any variances are highlighted and explained.

The third step is the followup action that is taken when an unacceptable variance is discovered. This is the most critical step of all; it is where the real profits are maintained and created.

That is the budgeting process in overview. A more detailed, step-by-step explanation is given below, and is summarized in Figure 7-1:

Step 1. Plan. A properly prepared budget grows from a well-defined business and marketing plan. Without a plan, the organization lacks direction. And without direction, the budget will be arbitrary.

The plan explains the current year's marketing goals. The forecast and budget are the financial expression of those goals, and they demonstrate that the goals are practical and can be achieved. The plan does not suggest that the numbers will fall exactly as shown, or even close. It does show that the plan is realistic and that it can be achieved. The numbers work.

Step 2. Goals. Setting goals as part of the plan is a logical and necessary step in the budgeting process. We should keep in mind that, in spite of the way things were done in the past, the worksheets filled with numbers are only part of the whole. Those columns and rows should represent the financial expression—and realization—of clearly stated goals.

Step 3. Assumptions. The key to budgeting is developing intelligent assumptions. For example, a sales forecast makes sense only when broken down by its component parts. So for example, if sales are generated by salespeople in the field, it makes sense to forecast based on assumptions about recruiting, attrition, and average production.

Expense budgets should be developed based on the components that logically constitute each category. The variable expense groups may vary with sales activity; overhead expenses are developed according to some logical pattern. Aban-

Figure 7-1. The budgeting process.

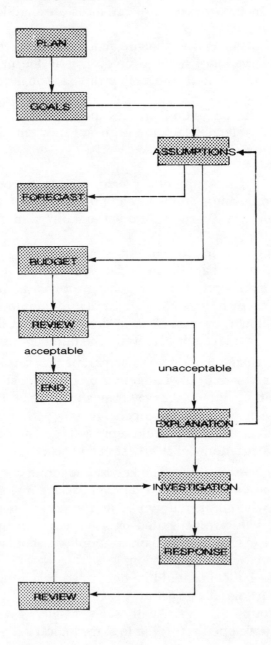

don the usual base for budgeting: percentage increases spread evenly throughout the year. These are useless to a need for analysis that will arise later in the year.

It also makes no sense to use the past, especially if the budget didn't work. Ask yourself, if last year's expenses exceeded budget, why are you using that outcome as the basis for the coming year? That's building in excessive expenses rather than creating controls to reduce the spending level.

Step 4. Sales forecast. The sales forecast should precede the cost and expense budget. Because your business and marketing plan is based on assumptions concerning an expanding market, the sales number should be developed as a first step. In many companies, expenses and sales are budgeting separately, which makes no sense at all.

Sales forecasts should be broken down by market, by month, and, if necessary, by sales office or other "unit of production" in your marketing arm. This enables you to later identify causes of variances.

Step 5. Budget. The cost and expense budget is based on intelligent assumptions related to the nature of the category. But in addition, the budgets will be directly affected by sales levels and timing. For example, if you believe that the summer months will experience a much higher than average sales volume, then it makes little sense to spread operating and variable expenses evenly throughout the year. You will then have timing differences in your budget. While these may not be major problems, they do cloud the important issues, often hiding real unfavorable variances from view.

Often overlooked in the budgeting process is the importance of cash-flow projections. Once you have completed a sales forecast and cost and expense budgets, you should next develop the year's cash-flow projection, as part of the test to see whether the plan will work.

What could go wrong? Cash flow will be affected by any number of situations. For example, what if you need to invest in capital assets? What if the new sales volume occurs on account, but related costs and expenses must be paid monthly?

What if your inventory level has to be doubled in the first quarter? All these events will demand additional capital. You need to ensure that you know where that capital will come from.

Step 6. Monthly review. This is a process of comparing actual to budgeted outcomes. The review should involve sales forecasts, cost and expense budgets, and cash-flow projections. Without the monthly review, you are not going through the budgeting process at all. Instead, you're letting the effort go to waste. Only by looking at the numbers can you tell whether the plan is working.

The review can be simplified to a great degree. This is most desirable. You don't want to keep a room full of busy managers and executives sitting for hours while going through a large volume of detail. All you need is a report showing each category in three columns: actual, budgeted, and the variance. If the variance is minor, no action is required. But if the variance is unacceptable, proceed to the next step.

Step 7. Explanation. Budget explanations create a lot of trouble for everyone. That's because in most cases, there is no logical assumption base. So what can you say about an expense that's higher than the budget?

In the traditional system, you might make an explanation sound good, without really saying anything at all. For example, "Actual expenses were 12 percent above last year's level. We estimated a 5 percent increase." This explanation says nothing at all about the *cause* of the variance; it only admits that the budget was too low, a fact that everyone already knows.

Unfortunately, this type of nonexplanation is so common that it's acceptable. We find ourselves coming up with new and novel ways of saying nothing, so that the corporate belief in budget review is satisfied.

A real explanation, in comparison, is based on an analysis between the components of actual spending (or income), and the components of the assumption base. With this method, precise reasons for a variance are quickly and easily identified. From there, it's a relatively easy step to take action, because a cause is now understood. A variance exists for only one of four reasons: (1) The budget did not anticipate something that happened. (2) The timing of the budget was in error, and will be offset in the future. (3) Internal accounting created the variance. This may include a coding error, an accrual, or an allocation not included in the budget. (4) The variance was predictable, but the original budget was changed arbitrarily from above or by the accounting department—in spite of well-documented assumptions.

Note in the diagram that the "explanation" step is referred back to the "assumptions" step. This is an essential component of the complete and effective budgeting system.

Step 8. Investigation. In some cases, the explanation cannot be filled in by the budget review meeting, because the person or department preparing the review (usually accounting) does not know the answer. At that point, an investigation is in order. It might be possible to assign the problem to one department, or it might be necessary to ask each manager to look into individual budget assumptions to identify the components of the variance.

Investigation is troublesome on a companywide basis. No one will want to take responsibility for explaining the variance, or for looking into it. As an unfortunate consequence, the accounting department ends up with the lion's share of budget-reporting duty. This means that, with or without your knowledge, *your* department could be criticized for a budgeting problem, even if you had nothing to do with developing that budget.

Step 9. Response. Once investigation is complete, some form of response is demanded. If an expense is running above a reasonable budget level, it should be brought under control. If the problem is strictly in one department, assignment of response is simple. However, it is more often a companywide problem and, again, no one will want to tackle the problem. So the accounting department again is given the responsibility and the power to respond and to solve. The power issue wouldn't be a problem in itself, except for the fact that you should want to control and answer for your own budget.

Step 10. Review. Once a problem is discovered and the process of correction is entered into, the review process begins. This is a year-round, never-ending, ongoing effort, one that should be instituted as a daily priority and as part of your routine. The idea of monitoring the budget is too often delegated, or thought of as an unpleasant and inconvenient demand on our time. Think of the control and review process not as manipulation of rows and columns of numbers, but as real and tangible events and financial consequences—that you can and should control as part of your job.

Review and monitoring—in other words, the exercise of control—can become a major source of profits. By reducing expenses and keeping their level as low as practical, you can increase the bottom line significantly.

FINDING YOUR ASSUMPTION BASE

How to begin developing an assumption base? Examine each type of cost or expense individually. Each contains its own specific attributes, and those attributes dictate the assumption base. Telephone expenses, for example, vary with the number of people in your department, pending rate increases, changes in the system you use, or the number of long distance calls your department makes each day. Office supplies can be broken down in a similar fashion; vendor price increases, employee usage, and purchasing patterns all dictate both the amount and the timing of expenses—at least for the purpose of assumption.

Remember this key point:

The purpose of developing assumptions is not to specifically guess at future expense levels, but to arrive at a reasonable standard against which the level of future expenses can be judged.

Some expenses can be budgeted from an assumption base dictated by contract, such as rent or equipment leases. For these types of expense, budgets are incredibly easy. Since there is no varying level to watch for, there is no need for control, nor is there an opportunity to reduce expenses through monitoring and correction. One exception: when market expansion could dictate additional facility or equipment leasing. In that instance, careful planning, control, and preapproval should be part of the plan and budget.

Other expenses are entirely unpredictable, and present a much more complicated budget challenge. For example, building or equipment maintenance cannot be predicted by amount or by timing. The only fair way to budget is to set up a reserve in the budget, and allow expenses to fall against that reserve. The reserve amount can be established based on historical maintenance patterns, the age of equipment on hand, or plans to replace equipment during the year.

Most expenses are controllable in one way or another. Telephone expenses can be controlled with policies regarding personal use. Office supply levels can be kept down with a centralized purchasing requisition system, locking up supply inventories, or demonstrated safeguards meant to curtail minor pilferage. Insurance expense levels are predictable based on anniversary dates of policies in force, plus known future requirements for additional coverage. In short, there are very few expenses that cannot be scientifically predicted, and for which a fair assumption base does not exist.

Developing appropriate assumptions might sound like a very time-consuming effort. You do need to create a documentation file for each and every category of expense in your department, develop the assumption, and then carry the result over to a worksheet. But this will not take any more time than doing your budget in the traditional manner. In fact, proper assumption-based budgeting will save time in the long run, for the reasons listed below and summarized in Figure 7-2:

• **Properly documented budgets reduce your task next year.** One of the greatest complaints about budgeting is that the process is long and tedious. It comes at the end of the year, often demanding overtime for everyone, and it drains your

Figure 7-2. Saving time in budgeting.

1. Properly documented budgets reduce your task next year.

2. Assumption—based budgeting leads to a higher rate of approval.

3. With documented assumptions in hand, you have a powerful weapon to resist arbitrary changes to your budget.

4. You will spend less time during the year struggling to come up with explanations for variances.

5. Budget revisions, if required, are more easily justified and executed.

6. Once you establish the appropriate assumption base for each account, new budgets can be prepared very quickly.

energy at a time when you're also trying to finish up other departmental matters. While assumption-based documentation might seem like just more paperwork, it is a form of departmental planning and organization. Thus, it saves time, cuts down on duplication of effort, and makes the entire task much easier—rather than harder.

• **Assumption-based budgeting leads to a higher rate of approval.** Budgets are also frustrating because, even with a carefully detailed budget, it might be necessary to revise the preliminary numbers several times before gaining final approval. With properly documented assumptions, you will be more likely to gain approval quickly, and with fewer revisions than before.

• **With documented assumptions in hand, you have a powerful weapon to resist arbitrary changes to your budget.** How often have you prepared a budget that seemed perfectly reasonable, only to have it cut without any justification? The only way to combat this problem is to present a budget that cannot be changed. If you have established complete documentation for the budget as presented, it will be impossible for anyone else to apply an across-the-board 10 percent cut. The budget simply wouldn't work as a consequence, and your documentation proves it.

• **You will spend less time during the year struggling to come up with explanations for variances.** Every department manager dreads being confronted with the monthly variance report. Even if no one reponds to the variance, the requirement is formidable if there is no assumption base. The problem disappears when actual expenses can be evaluated in light of the assumption base. A simple analysis shows where the budget missed the mark, or where actual expenses demand more control.

• **Budget revisions, if required, are more easily justified and executed.** It might seem that, just as you complete the current year's budget, worksheets arrive for the six-month revision. While the policy of midyear revisions should be questioned most critically, many organizations continue to waste time developing detailed budgets that will never be put to good use. Without assumptions for each account, revisions may require as much work as the original budget.

No one likes revisions because, like original budgets, there is never a "good" time to do them. But you can make revisions much more quickly by going through your original assumptions, modifying them based on what the first six months have revealed, and recommending one of two changes in response:

Either tighten controls on spending, or revise the budget for items overlooked in the original version.

• **Once you establish the appropriate assumption base for each account, new budgets can be prepared very quickly.** Perhaps the one reason budgets demand so much analysis time is that we don't learn from past successes or failures. The past year's budget should not be abandoned automatically, but it usually is. Once the year is ended, how often do you look back at last year's worksheets?

If you have used assumption-based documentation to build the current year's budget, the actual outcome—in comparison to your estimation work—is a very revealing document. You can improve your budgeting technique, your accuracy rate, and your sense of timing, by referring to the previous budget while preparing a new one.

CREATING YOUR SOURCE FILE

You would think that the budgeting task would shrink with time. That's what happens with most other tasks. But instead, it seems that when budgeting season opens, we all grit our teeth for long weeks of endless work and revision. We accept the fact that budgeting always takes a lot of time and involves a lot of pain. It doesn't have to be that way.

Why repeat the process every six to twelve months, when you *can* improve procedures, cut back on duplication, and make budgeting an efficient and valid form of analysis? By building a source file of information, you will be able to save time next year and, perhaps, even eliminate budget-related overtime in your department.

Source file information should include:

• Business and marketing plans
• Last year's budget and budget worksheets
• The sales forecast
• Account analysis for your department

- Information on vendor pricing trends
- Trend analysis developed in your department
- Analysis of expense-reduction measures you have created and put into effect
- Analysis of expense trends related to employee usage

All these, plus any other relevant intelligence, can be brought together in your budget file. With the collective data you accumulate, you will be able to develop and improve upon assumptions used for each category of expense.

The richer the file, the better. You can never have too much information with which to prepare your budget. Of course, an overwhelming volume of material would inhibit rather than forward your budget effort. But you are unlikely to face this problem. If your company is typical, you will be more likely to suffer a shortage of information than an excess.

A final note on the entire budgeting process: It is an obvious statistical reality that, when predicting a likely future, the further out you go, the less dependable the numbers become. So a twelve-month budget is much less dependable than a six-month budget. Put more precisely, the eleventh and twelfth months are far less likely to be accurate than the fifth and sixth months.

With these realities in mind, most companies budget for a full year, and then undergo a full-blown six-month revision. This makes no sense. An alternative, at least for internal control purposes, is to budget for only the next six months.

Chapter 8

Supporting Your Budget

Filling out worksheets is only the first battle in the budget war. Unless you prefer to be a passive victim of what others expect from the political side of budgeting, you need to prepare yourself. This means being ready to support your position and your budget, line by line if necessary. Fortunately, analysis and documentation provide you with the tools you need.

Just as corporate profits reflect more than just a series of numbers on the page, budgets reflect much more, too. A properly conceived budget grows from the plan, where short-term goals are developed and explained. Reaching goals involves coordinating capital and human resources in a singular effort. Monitoring progress and trends (both financial and human) requires development of effective internal systems, through both the budgeting process and the leadership process.

Our concern is with the support side, the routines needed to make your budget work. You do, however, need to be prepared to answer critics and to defend your department's position as expressed in the budget you have prepared. It is not enough to take a stand or even to make a statement of protest. You also need to be ready to come forward with a more practical solution. Budgets based on guesswork are not worth the time they take to prepare. Budgets based on analysis can be used as important profit-generating tools, not only for the whole company, but for your department as well.

MERGING ASSUMPTIONS AND NUMBERS

The first step following development of assumptions is to translate those assumptions into numbers. Now, it might seem that the numbers are actually part of the assumption. To an extent, that's true. However, there is a big difference between the premise (the reasoning that goes into the assumption) and the numbers (the financial representation of that premise). Merging the assumption with the numbers is a fairly simple step. It involves expressing the belief in financial terms.

What do other people say about budgeting in specific accounts? You have probably heard a statement like this: "It's just about impossible to accurately budget office supplies, because so many things go into the account." That's just the point. When an account is complex to track and pin down, assumption-based budgeting works best. With a series of assumptions about the nature of the expense, you will be able to develop the numbers that go along with it.

> *Example:* In researching the coming year's budget, you discover that your major supplier is planning a 5 percent price increase as of the first of the year. In response, you plan to add 5 percent to the budget for all items purchased from that store. A possible alternative is to compare prices of other suppliers. Or you could look for opportunities to purchase in bulk and take advantage of discounts.

> *Example:* You check supplies, and discover that you will be running out of file folders, photocopy paper, and several other items early in the year. You budget for a full year's supply to take advantage of discounts suppliers offer; the budget for these purchases must be carefully planned to avoid timing variances. This situation presents another opportunity for savings: Perhaps, by centralizing supply purchases, you will be able to effect big savings on a companywide basis. It's worth investigating.

These simple examples demonstrate a very significant point: The process of preparing a budget might well point out ways to save money. This is a key benefit of preparing budgets properly.

STARTING AT THE DEPARTMENTAL LEVEL

Budgets are generally thought of in companywide terms. In many cases, individual departments are left out of the process, or are limited to filling in worksheets at the preliminary stages only. The accounting department ends up doing much of the consolidation work. So, even though department managers are in the best position to explain their budgets, they aren't even in the meeting when the decision is made.

I suggest a new approach. Each department should be keenly involved in its own budget. This means making sure that reasonable requests are honored and not arbitrarily removed. It also means offering opinions about reporting and monitoring procedures; helping to identify methods for controlling expenses and responding to unfavorable variances; and having a say about budgeting decisions that will affect you and your department directly.

Begin by instituting a more reasonable approach to budgeting at the departmental level. You cannot impose your ideas on the organization at large, of course. But you can demonstrate ideas that save time and lead to greater profits. That gets the attention of the decision makers.

Some suggestions for instituting the departmental-level budgeting procedure are given below and summarized in Figure 8-1:

• **Document everything thoroughly.** If you mean to put sensible budgeting procedures into effect at the departmental level, you may count on one thing: You will be challenged by others. Traditional-thinking people will resist change, no matter how much sense it makes. If you claim things work better with the new procedure and you then try to get others to adopt it, be prepared to prove your point. Then be prepared for

Figure 8-1. Instituting the departmental budget.

```
1. Document everything thoroughly.

2. Cross–reference to assumptions.

3. Challenge arbitrary change.

4. Ask to be included at the final
   point of decision about your
   budget.

5. Document imposed changes.

6. Organize a budget file.

7. Invite comparisons.
```

outright refusal, even in the face of obvious logic. You will be expected to establish a paper trail for each and every conclusion reached in the departmental budget. Even with that, you will be under suspicion as one who suggested a change.

• **Cross-reference to assumptions.** It might not be enough to demonstrate to others that your departmental budget is thoroughly prepared. Think of your assumptions as proof of what you claim. Refer and cross-reference your numbers according to what the assumptions bear out. Don't be afraid to use this system extensively. Analysis, when done thoroughly and properly, is the most convincing argument you can present.

Example: When you present your proposed departmental budget to the review committee, the first response is to reject it—"Too high." However, you present a number of arguments aimed at making a case that your budget is not only reasonable; it's also a lean and properly conceived budget. You use statistical summaries of volume and expense trends to make your point, referring back to the assumptions to show how your budget was cut back and trimmed.

• **Challenge arbitrary change.** The status quo in budgeting seems to be this: First, each department develops its own budget, using worksheets supplied by the accounting department. This stage entails weeks of work, including a lot of overtime. When the budget is submitted, someone else—an executive, the accounting department, or the budget committee—reduces the department's budget by 10 percent. No reason is given. Then when unfavorable variances appear a few months later, the department manager is called upon to explain why the department is spending too much money.

Arbitrary changes make no sense, and should be fought. Well-researched assumptions are your best weapon against such changes. If you can make your case with a series of assumptions, then arbitrary changes cannot be supported.

• **Ask to be included at the final point of decision about your budget.** You have every right to be consulted at the point a decision is made about your department's budget. Ask to be included. Remind the decision makers that you will have to live with the final budget all year. If you are to be held accountable for it, you also expect to be directly involved in its development and outcome.

More managers would insist on attending these critical budget meetings if only they realized what occurs. In the pressure to reduce expense estimates, arbitrary changes are made against departmental budgets. But too often managers, tired of the entire endless process, are just glad it's out of their hands.

• **Document imposed changes.** What do you do when, in spite of your efforts, your budget is changed without your participation? Document your case. Keep complete records of your original budget and the one that is imposed upon you. Then, when you're called on to explain large unfavorable variances, begin with your original budget; then document the arbitrary changes imposed upon you; and let some or all of the variance be assigned to the changes you were forced to accept.

• **Organize a budget file.** Start saving budget-related memos, letters, directives, decisions, and worksheets. Everything that goes into your budget should be organized into a permanent file. This will prove invaluable later, when variances come up. It will also help establish a better and faster procedure next year.

> *Example:* Your budget shows substantial negative variances in several accounts. You have tactfully referred to a last-minute reduction imposed by the accounting department, but memories of those events have faded and you're being stuck with full responsibility. You refer to your file and pull out a memo from accounting, instructing you to reduce all expense categories by 10%.

• **Invite comparisons.** Ultimately, the best possible case you can make for improved budgeting procedures is comparison. If your ideas work better than other, more traditional ones, ask others to look at the facts. Allow comparisons to be made, and the better procedure will show up as the obvious way to go.

The department is the best place to start making a difference. You are on familiar ground, and you're an expert in the matters affecting you. By good example, you will eventually influence other departments and, perhaps, the entire company.

Chapter 9

Variance Reporting

When you consider that budgeting is nothing more than the best possible informed guess about the future, you have to expect some variance to arise. It's inevitable. But it is not a sign of failure. The variance itself is not the problem. Variances can be positives if used correctly—to discover and reverse unfavorable trends.

When an unfavorable variance does come up (and it will), it is not necessarily cause for alarm. It's simply a signal that the time has come to fix a problem. Too often, the variance itself becomes the bad news. So instead of fixing what the budget reveals, we find ourselves covering up, writing acceptable explanations, or blaming outside influences. The only real consequence of this is to neutralize the budget and bypass its intended control features.

THE TRADITIONAL APPROACH

The traditional approach to variance reporting is flawed, simply because it does not allow you to fix problems. The traditional approach includes these myths:

• **Positive variances are always good news.** In an expense account, the negative variance says that you spent more money than you were supposed to. Therefore, the argument continues, a positive variance must be good news. And that thinking is not correct. Variances are signs that your "best guess" did not occur, and there are reasons for that.

Remember the purpose of budgeting: to predict a likely and acceptable future. A variance—in either direction—is the symptom of a problem. A positive variance could point to a flawed budgeting procedure that's overly conservative, timing problems in setting the current budget, or extraordinary results from the exercise of controls. Any of these indicates a compelling need for further analysis to identify where the problem is and what to do about it.

• **Negative variances should be explained away.** The value of the negative variance is that it leads to corrective action and, as a result, higher profits. Negative variances should never simply be explained away. The explanation should not only tell what went wrong, but should also indicate the immediate course of action that should be taken, and by whom.

• **A six-month revision is the best cure for this period's chronic variance problem.** Revised budgets are coverups. Imagine how more carefully everyone would be forced to budget if there could be no midyear revisions. In fact, why budget for the entire year, since we already know it's going to be inaccurate? Why not just do a new budget every six months and forego the exercise of revision? It makes sense, and is an idea worth suggesting to your company's decision makers.

The only argument favoring full-year budgeting with mid-year revisions is that, especially for publicly traded companies, the budget corresponds with the fiscal year. Analysts and stockbrokers want to know what management expects during the coming year. As valid an argument as this is, it's really a planning issue. The budget is an internal document, and should be done as practically and usefully as possible. The full-year requirement can be taken care of in a different forum.

What Variances Are Significant?

In deciding to track down both positive and negative variances and analyze their causes, you must address another question:

Will you explain every variance, or only those that are significant? It doesn't make sense to explain every account, when
some will show variances of only a few dollars. Only the
"significant" variance needs explanation. Too much unimpor-
tant detail is time consuming in preparation and review, and
distracts from the value of a variance report.

How do you make the distinction? You need to set a policy
(or, more precisely, ask top management to decide upon a
policy and then impose it on each department) concerning the
definition of a significant variance. This definition should apply
to positive *and* negative variances, and should involve both the
amount and the percentage of variance. For example, you
could decide that a "significant" variance is one that varies 10
percent or more from the budget, when the amount is $1,000
or more.

The amount and percentage should be modified up or
down based on the volume of income, costs, and expenses,
and on the outcome of the variance report. You should be able
to spot a truly significant variance by simply looking at the
amounts and percentages as they fall.

DETERMINING REPORTING PERIODS

One point you must address in setting budget variance reporting policy is frequency. Should you report monthly variances
only, or year to date? The argument in favor of monthly
variance reporting is that you won't need to repeat explanations from previous periods. This is true. But year-to-date
reporting still makes more sense.

Under the monthly variance reporting method, only each
month's budget and actual are compared. The system is clean,
as previous year-to-date variances will not be included. However, it is common for timing differences to pop up from one
month to another, and year-to-date reporting takes care of this
problem in many instances.

A big problem with monthly reporting is that previous,

unresolved variances fall between the cracks—unless there is some followup procedure to investigate and correct a problem. Anyone who has been involved with budgets already knows how difficult it is to add this amount of bureaucracy to an already paper-intensive procedure.

The important thing is to *know* why a variance exists and to take corrective action, if possible.

By the time you come to the end of a budget period, having to summarize a large number of variances belonging to past months may be quite irritating. But remember that the purpose of the budget is to set a measurable standard, and not to guess the future precisely. The problem of outstanding and uncorrected variances only emphasizes the point that no one can really predict the future. A best guess is acceptable; an informed best guess is extraordinary.

GIVING THE BUDGET A NEW PURPOSE

Variances, properly used, can give budgets a new purpose. Companies need to look on variance reporting not just as a means for calling managers to account for problems, but a way of turning that budgeting process into a profit center. Suggesting this perspective to top management will turn heads and gain attention. It is a good idea and it works.

There are a number of steps you can take to achieve the benefits intended from the budgeting process, and you will see tangible results at once:

• **Respond to discovered variances.** In some companies, a monthly variance report is prepared, variances carefully researched, and explanations developed diligently. Then, everyone files their copy of the report, and nothing is done. This is a lost opportunity.

Take a different approach. When you discover that an account in your department has a significant variance, take immediate action. Identify the cause of the problem and fix it.

If the variance is significant in either direction, it deserves a careful look. And when you find the answer, your task has just begun. From there, you need to decide what actions are appropriate; then you need to follow through and take those actions.

• **Build control ideas into assumptions.** One idea that is too often overlooked is that of building control ideas into the budget itself. If you think of budgeting as a function outside what you actually do, then you have missed the point. In fact, budgeting should be (but rarely is) an ongoing exercise in control.

Typically, the budget comes up only at the end of the month, when a variance report is prepared; or at the end of the fiscal year, when you're reminded that, once again, it's time to stay late and start filling out worksheets. But suppose you have a problem keeping expenses down, so you correct the problem. The budget assumption for that expense category might be the logical starting point for getting your accounts under control, assuming your control ideas work.

Example: Your office supply purchases consistently run above budget; no matter what, you just can't seem to bring the account under control. Then you come up with an idea for an improved purchasing system. You believe it will reduce supply expenses by 10% per month. It might be arbitrary, and it might not occur. But at least the intention is stated and expressed in financial terms.

• **Modify to correct, not to avoid problems.** What's the point in responding to a problem in such a way that it just returns again month after month? It makes more sense to correct that problem once and for all. Unfortunately, budgeting priorities might prevent you from achieving this.

How should you respond? Get in there and solve the problem. If the budget is reasonable but employees are spending more than they should, put a preapproval system in place. If the budget is simply wrong and the spending level is right, document that fact as part of your explanation. In either case, don't let the problem go. And don't complicate the real reasons for the problem by providing an acceptable answer that doesn't really say anything. That only prevents anyone from knowing what should be done.

EXPLANATIONS STATED AS GOALS

Analysis may be thought of as a process of manipulating numbers. But that's only the outward part of analysis. Properly used, analysis is also a dynamic system for expressing departmental or corporate goals.

When it comes to explanations of budget variances, you have one of the best opportunities for demonstrating how well your company or department is reaching its goals. This assumes, of course, that the budgeting process was developed correctly: The plan documented goals, which were in turn expressed in terms of the budget.

Example: Your company is working from a six-month budget for market expansion. The sales forecast called for a 30% increase in a short time. That goal has been achieved. However, at the same time, your department forecast a telephone expense at about the same level as last year. At the time your budget was prepared, you believed this was possible. Now, you have discovered that as volume grows, so does telephone usage.

Whether or not expenses can be brought into line with the budget, the variance provides a chance to bring the goal to the attention of the decision makers. The point here: The budget was either realistic or not. And variances display how goals within the plan are working. In this instance, it seems there was an oversight. Telephone expenses might logically rise when volume goes up. But what if the department is not directly involved in sales or customer contact? Why would telephone expenses go up in this case? It could be that in periods of higher volume, internal controls are relaxed. Employees, sensing that the company is prospering, receive a new message: It is no longer important to control expenses. So across the spending board, controls fall by the wayside.

What can you do if your company has not prepared a plan, or if a plan exists but no specific goal statements are included? Assume responsibility for setting goals for yourself. They can be expressed in general terms, and then set up as standards through your assumptions and budget. Then, when variances appear, your explanation refers back to the original goal.

A key point:

> When you set goals and then track them through the budget, you have a much better chance of improving profits and avoiding negative variances.

Having the goal helps you to monitor the expense with greater awareness. Just knowing what you hope to achieve makes the entire budgeting process more significant, and more rewarding. Setting goals also enables you to take control. As your own analyst, you need and deserve control. But when it comes to budgeting, too many of us feel frustrated and helpless, a small part of a larger machinery that no one really knows how to operate.

SAVING MONEY FOR THE COMPANY

One primary goal for every manager should be saving money for the company. This is the ever-present task of *all* employees. That means adopting a concern for corporate profits.

People in direct touch with customers tend to think of top-line growth as the logical way to increase sales. And that belief is entirely valid. Higher sales are essential to higher profits, assuming that costs and expenses are also held in check. But only a small number of departments are involved directly with sales and with customers. Without direct customer contact, how can you improve profits? The answer is by holding down expenses; and that is achieved in only one way: establishing and monitoring internal controls, one of the most important of which is budgeting itself.

Internal controls are generally thought of as completely separate from budgeting. For most employees, "controls" means telephone logs, requisitioning systems, preapproval rules for expenses, and locking up of valuable inventory. All these are highly visible forms of control, but there are others: cash-handling procedures, a departmental petty cash fund, a supervisor being required to initial check requests, or a manager's daily meeting with staff.

Now consider the budget and the underlying process. This is one of the most critical internal controls in any company. The budget, in fact, is your primary financial control. The information that you get from variances can help you save money for the company in very direct and immediate ways. Ignoring variances is like failing to collect money that's due from a customer, or leaving the electricity on day and night in a large plant. These things cost money. So does failing to use the budget.

In those companies where budgets and variances are taken very seriously, how do people react differently than in other companies? Some of the major differences are listed below and summarized in Figure 9-1:

• **Variances are acted upon when found.** A basic step in budgeting is to act on a variance when it shows up. This is very obvious but, unfortunately, it's done only rarely. The problem almost always comes down to top management's failure to enforce the idea that controls should work, or that new controls should be created as new problems arise.

• **Negatives are reversed and positives are protected.** Trends emerge from budgeting and, with analysis, are easily discovered. In companies that succeed with budgets, the negatives are attacked and reversed vigorously. And the positive trends that emerge are protected from change.

• **The process is reviewed month to month.** Budgeting, to

Figure 9-1.   Guidelines: appropriate responses to variances.

1. Variances are acted upon when found.

2. Negatives are reversed and positives are protected.

3. The process is reviewed month to month.

4. Budgeting itself is a lean and efficient process.

5. Revisions are not undertaken to hide errors, but to improve controls.

6. Everyone keeps sight of planning goals.

many people, is an annual or semiannual pilgrimage to the land of accounting. Everyone stays late and pays their respects to the columnar pad, balancing and footing columns and rows of numbers. Then, you have four to five months off. In a well-managed company, the initial steps are assumption-based, which adds value throughout the year as well as saving everyone a lot of time. The monthly review, however, is where the real budgeting controls take place. Filling out the worksheets is only a representation of the standard. Actual outcome is where the standard is tested.

• **Budgeting itself is a lean and efficient process.** Another thing about companies that use budgeting properly: The initial process and the monthly review are executed in a shorter time than in companies that don't budget well. Because budgeting is done the right way, the political aspects go away, and arbitrary changes are eliminated. Then, at monthly reviews, the interest is in eliminating negatives, not in covering up a budgeting error.

• **Revisions are not undertaken to hide errors, but to improve controls.** When budgets must be revised, it should be to improve internal controls and save money. In fact, in companies that budget well, either revisions are not done at all, or they are limited to the corrective variety. Unfortunately, in many companies, budget revisions are opportunities to cover up the fact that the original budget was inadequate.

• **Everyone keeps sight of planning goals.** Finally, companies that budget well base all considerations on the plan and the goals that are expressed within that plan. The budget is not just columns and rows of numbers on a worksheet, and a monthly report that glosses over what's really happening.

THE PROFIT-CENTERED MANAGER

The manager who prepares budgets from logical assumptions and then carefully tracks variances and responds is directly involved in making goals happen. This leads directly to higher profits. The manager who is able to put the new budgeting idea into practice will budget more accurately, gain greater control and, to a large extent, will be able to actually control the future.

The idea of "control" in this context should be examined carefully. To some, the corporate version of control translates to procedures and approval; to others, it's a political influence issue. We mean neither of these when discussing control of the future.

The profit-centered manager understands that the future is uncertain; but that with proper budgeting, a range of outcomes can be made to happen. That range is desirable because it leads to corporate profits, healthy cash flow, and realization of goals—not only for the company, but for the staff of the department and the manager personally. Budgeting, when combined with informed leadership and fair treatment of employees, is a valuable tool for creating, maintaining, and even determining levels of profit.

Chapter 10

Planning the Human Side

You might take complete command of the numbers, become a shrewd analyst, and master the tricks of the accounting trade. But unless you also understand how to analyze the needs of your department in terms of people, analysis is not enough. Anticipating future labor requirements is more elusive than many other trends.

This is a flaw of many numbers-oriented managers. They know the numbers, but don't understand how to plan for their own department's needs in the short-term future. Analysis can help you determine future needs on the basis of work versus available people; it can also help you to protect your department from excessive demands on a limited resource pool.

DEFENDING YOUR STAFFING NEEDS

Labor demands might occur seasonally or respond to easily identified external factors. For example, if your department's work varies with sales volume, then a forecasted increase in volume will also spell more work for your department. This is the clue you need to identify the best methods of analysis on the human side.

There may be any number of external factors at work, depending on your department and attributes of the work you do. It is difficult to imagine a department working entirely in isolation, without any external factors involved. Some possible factors other than sales volume are listed as follows:

Factor	Typical Departments
Number of employees in other departments	Personnel
Seasonal changes in business levels	Accounting
Number of customers	Service
Number of field salespeople	Marketing

How can you use analysis to anticipate labor requirements in the near future? Historical information helps to a degree and should be incorporated in your analysis. In addition, new systems, ideas for increasing efficiency, or new influences (such as a change to your department's overall range of responsibility) will also modify the historical file.

If you have done your analysis, and are able to use the results of analysis to make your case convincingly, you can effectively counter the popular arguments against giving you the increases in staffing that you need. The popular arguments and the best responses are:

• **"It's not in the budget."** It's amazing that budgets are referred to so often, even by those who never use them for their intended purpose. The budget is, indeed, a political routine when it's used as an excuse to avoid the real issues. You do not have to accept that answer, especially if your request if fair and reasonable.

Consider this response: "If the budget wasn't the reason, would you have a problem with my request? And if so, why?" Now you corner the individual and force the issue. Don't attack; that would be politically unwise. Once you lead the person through the logic of your request, it will become very obvious that the limitations of the budget have nothing to do with reason. Your idea makes sense to the bottom-line thinker. It will increase profits and reduce expenses. It will make processes flow more smoothly or meet expansion demands as they occur. No decision maker can ignore such benefits. So your job in a meeting or presentation is to appeal to the issues the decision maker cares about.

- **"Your department has already grown too rapidly."** This is a ludicrous reason for turning down a reasonable request. If a department has grown out of control and the manager simply doesn't do the job well, then this argument could stand. But the excuse is often given to the most diligent and competent managers, in which case it makes no sense at all.

The solution? Anticipate this reply to your request, especially if you have already increased staff during the last three years. Then prepare an analysis showing that staff increases have saved money, that volume of work has outpaced staff increases, and that your actions saved the company money. Furthermore, demonstrate that hiring more people will produce more profit than expense. These are the arguments that win.

- **"No one else is asking for more staff."** Another poor excuse! But this one is also used widely. So be prepared for it. Prove that, while everyone else is content to take on more work, lose efficiency, and sacrifice quality, you intend to take the opposite path. You want to maintain quality, deliver work on time and accurately, and ensure that, directly or indirectly, the customer will be well served.

- **"Management wants a hiring freeze."** Hiring or salary freezes, like budgets, are more often than not excuses passed on from top management to the rank and file. In some cases, freezes are necessary, but when they're used to deny a reasonable and potentially profitable request, it's a case of burying one's head in the sand.

Counter the argument by presenting a sensible idea: First, ask why the freeze. The answer is always the same: because profits aren't high enough. Then complete the chain of logic by explaining that your idea will do just that. By hiring more people, you will be ready to demonstrate, the company will increase profits.

SOLVING THE WORKLOAD PROBLEM

Virtually every manager constantly struggles with the problem of workload. If you're overstaffed, it costs the company money and you have employees waiting around idly. When people are not kept busy, their morale falls and it leads to trouble. But if you're understaffed, you could have morale problems, too. People feel that too much is expected of them. The pressure is constant. So quality suffers, the error rate grows, attitudes decline. How can you strike the best possible balance? In fact, analysis of workload and employee productivity can help you to maintain the balance between efficient budgets and a comfortable amount of work.

ASKING FOR STAFF EXPANSION

One of the most challenging fights you will have in your career as a nonaccountant manager is getting approval for staff expansion. You need to use the numbers to your advantage and to show by analysis that you understand the issues. But because you are not an accountant, your conclusions—even when you can prove them with facts developed from analysis—will always be suspect, at least until you gain the reputation as a shrewd and insightful analyst.

How do you fight the mistaken belief that no one but accountants can accurately analyze numbers or develop a meaningful analysis? The only way is by presenting your facts, subjecting them to review, and proving your point—not only once, but again and again, until the idea gets across that your figures are dependable, and your conclusions are accurate. In this instance, words won't make your case. But consistent results will.

A most critical point to remember: If you want to make the impression on others, especially accountants, that you can perform accurate and meaningful analysis, be sure your numbers are right. Your conclusions, based on an interpretation of the numbers, should be indisputable and acceptable to the accounting brains in your company—and not only on your terms, but on theirs too. Remember, though, that one math error in your reports will bring the entire matter into question. Once someone loses confidence in your accuracy, it might take months, even years, to gain it back.

Pleasing accountants is a fairly simple matter. They don't require a lot. In most instances, they ask for only a short list of attributes in anything you put on the table:

- *Accuracy.* Accountants like the numbers to add up. Because you're a nonaccountant, your addition will be suspect. And because they are accountants, they *will* check.
- *Profit orientation.* The accountant thinks in terms of numbers, and the most impressive number is the bottom line. So if you're asking for additional staff, address the profit issue.
- *Organization.* Accountants have logical minds. They like the numbers to be balanced, and in the right place. Use the right terminology, cross reference, and present your information neatly. Don't forget to leave enough of a trail for anyone to follow, and don't present any numbers that can't be verified and explained in detail.

Some guidelines for proving your point are listed below and summarized in Figure 10-1:

- **Always refer just to the facts.** Present information in the most fact-based method possible. Leave out hunches, intuition, emotion, and anything else that is nontangible—even when you know you're right. Be ready to prove everything and use *only* the facts to make your point.

Figure 10-1. Guidelines: proving your point.

```
1. Always refer just to the facts.

2. Use accounting information as
   support.

3. Make it easy for someone else
   to find the facts in your report.

4. Back up summarized information
   with very clear worksheets
   showing the details.

5. Use actual numbers in place of
   estimates whenever possible.
```

• **Use accounting information as support.** The accounting department itself provides a wealth of supporting information for a number of analytical reports you will present. Refer to forecasts, financial statements and reports, and historical information found in the books and accounts. If the accountant challenges your information on the basis of accounting data, you have a strong counterargument. Your data came from *their* own files.

• **Make it easy for someone else to find the facts in your report.** Take a little time to organize your reports very methodically. Accountants respond well to organized information; they will be more willing to study your report if you make it extremely easy to audit your information. The most compelling argument you can make is full disclosure of your facts and assumptions.

• **Back up summarized information with very clear worksheets showing the details.** The summary page of your report should include as little detail as possible. State your case and your assumptions, put down the request or recommendation, and conclude. Then tie each assumption to more detailed information in the body of the report. This is the most efficient way to lead someone from your request through the assumptions, and point by point, to the proof of what you claim.

Analysis is a powerful tool when used in this way. You will need to develop analytical techniques to take a point through the numbers and to an understandable presentation. You will also need to do so in such a way that someone else can follow your train of thought.

Even when the logic is very clear to you, it's important to assume that someone else will not want to struggle to comprehend your ideas. Make it easy. Don't expect anyone else to work as hard as you. Be willing to lay out the steps in the process, and to prove beyond any doubt that you are right. Even though more than one answer might apply, convince your audience that *your* answer is the best one.

• **Use actual numbers in place of estimates whenever possible.** Accountants are big on credibility. Even so, they themselves often need to use estimates. As a general rule of thumb, the more estimates included in analysis, the less dependable the conclusions. Avoid estimates whenever actual numbers are available, even if that means having to spend more time to get them.

Use the same approach accountants use. When you must use estimates, develop them in the most conservative manner possible. If you anticipate a 30 percent increase in work in your department as a consequence of higher sales volume, base your analysis on a 15 or 20 percent increase.

In every analysis you present and in every presentation you give, address the issue of increased sales and profits. Appeal to the marketing mind of the decision maker. Show how a decision or action will raise the value of stock, increase profits, or lead to new expansion possibilities. Failing any of that, show how costs and expenses can be cut by responding to your suggestions.

That is one half of the approach. The other half is appealing to the accounting mind. The decision makers in your company depend on accountants and other financial advisers, because information they supply is considered to be consistently accurate and dependable. You market yourself and your department by demonstrating that you, even though a nonaccountant, can be depended upon for the same level of accurate and meaningful information, without fail.

Chapter 11

Using Analysis in Meetings

The day arrives when every manager—prepared or not—is called upon to enter a meeting and present a report. Whether it's oral or written, you are on the line during the brief time you're given to lay out the facts. That makes your time in the limelight critical.

You put your entire reputation on the line whenever you speak out in a meeting. Knowing this, some people would prefer to attend meetings but say nothing. This is wasted time and opportunity. It is better to become an active participant in the meeting, and to make a difference in the outcome of tasks and assignments.

The decision makers at the meeting have an unwavering agenda. They are concerned with profit. The question is always there, whether stated or not. So in presenting your case, be sure your analysis addresses their issue as well as yours. Show how a decision will affect profits.

Presenting profit-oriented reports is not the whole story, as you well know. Decisions are made and alliances are formed or broken on the basis of complex but unspoken rules. The political undercurrent of your organization is perhaps more of a determining factor in your success than on-target analysis will ever be. To survive the political maze of corporate life, you need to develop the skills of a manager-diplomat. In addition to becoming a master in the art of analysis, you also need to gently prod others and to convince them that your conclusions are inescapably right.

REALITIES OF DECISION MAKING

The above does not imply that the decision maker is always without direction. However, it is important to recognize a few realities concerning analysis and its parts: forecasting, risk identification, and the decision-making process as listed here and summarized in Figure 11-1:

• **Decisions about the future are based mostly on historical information.** You already know that most decisions are based on intelligence about the past. Do your best to dig out dependable past information, then look for current information to supplement what you already have in hand from the past.

• **We know nothing about the future.** The future is always uncertain. No matter how much time or effort you put into forecasting and no matter how thorough or scientific your analysis, it's still only an estimate. Your analysis might be an extremely detailed and scientific study of the past, be supplemented with the best current research available, and take into consideration a number of scenarios—and still be way off track.

Thorough analysis does not predict the future; it only identifies and supports degrees of risk, likely outcomes, and possibilities. It is primarily based on a study of trends, and supported with whatever else you can gather in the way of facts. Decision makers need this information.

• **Decisions are sometimes made not in the best interests of the company, a department, or even the decision maker.** You have submitted a written proposal to management, suggesting changes in procedures that will save the company more than $15,000 per year in overhead expenses. Your research has established this beyond any doubt. However, your recommendation is turned down.

Figure 11-1. Realities of the decision-making process.

1. Decisions about the future are based mostly on historical information.

2. We know nothing about the future.

3. Decisions are sometimes made not in the best interests of the company, a department, or even the decision maker.

4. Decision makers do not always have identical risk tolerance levels.

5. There may be a host of factors affecting the decision maker beyond what you know.

6. Internal politics might play a major role in how decisions are made.

7. Human beings make mistakes.

Why would a decision maker turn down an idea that would save money? There could be many reasons, not all of them logical. For example, the savings might come from reduction in payroll, which might be unpopular with another manager. It could also involve admitting past errors in judgment, which the decision maker might not be willing to admit.

What should you do in a case like this? File your report away and wait. Observe and listen. Your chance will come around again. For now, accept the fact that issues beyond your immediate sphere are at work, other people are involved, and political considerations are complicating the real issues. In such situations, you don't want to be directly in the line of fire.

• **Decision makers do not always have identical risk tolerance levels.** The decision maker with whom you communicate today will express a given tolerance for risk. The one you meet with tomorrow may not have the same attitude. Recognize that each decision maker is an individual. Even if their environments are identical, they will react in different ways to suggestions.

• **There may be a host of factors affecting the decision maker beyond what you know.** The decision maker's range of vision is probably much broader than yours, so it's wise to respect a decision, even if it makes no sense from your point of view.

Suppose you make a recommendation that will help you reduce your department's staff by 25 percent over the next two years. At the weekly management meeting the vice president quickly rejected the idea and then changed the subject. Perhaps the vice president is aware of certain secret negotiations that will open up a whole new product line. If that goes through, your department will have to expand, rather than cut back.

• **Internal politics might play a major role in how decisions are made.** Not only are decision makers influenced by outside circumstances or individuals, they are also sensitive to the full political environment in the company. A middle manager is exposed directly to middle management politics, and may be only vaguely aware of the political climate on different rungs of the corporate ladder.

Never assume that what you see is the entire story. The report you submit, based on the analysis you carefully prepared, might make sense. But politics at the decision maker's level, rather than at yours, will ultimately determine whether your ideas win approval.

• **Human beings make mistakes.** Even if the various outside influences and pressures are not present, the decision maker reviewing your ideas is prone to errors, like the rest of us. If your analysis is thorough and complete and if it does prove what you claim, then the rate of acceptance of your ideas definitely will go up. However, don't assume that it will be automatic.

You might have to be willing to diplomatically educate the decision maker. This is normal operating procedure. Don't expect an executive to know *your* issues as well as you do; that's not realistic. And don't be too harsh a judge when the decision maker demonstrates ignorance of the way you and your department operate. Your job is to explain the facts clearly and directly, so that the right decision can be made. Don't assume the executive's job is to understand what you're facing, unless you explain it.

Meetings are dangerous waters, in one respect. If you are not prepared, the impression you make will be negative and it will be difficult to change. But if you prepare and make a positive impression, then you will be on your way to gaining the reputation you want.

PRESENTING MULTIPLE POSSIBILITIES

So, there you are, with the results of an analysis. Your trend is clearly identified, and the direction is clear. But what does it really mean? You think the outcome is positive but, as you've just seen, others might have a much different point of view. For completely valid reasons, your positive outcome could be a disaster to the department across the hall. Whenever you enter a meeting with plans to present your analysis, be prepared to revise your thinking entirely. In fact, be prepared to have *all* your assumptions challenged by others. If you want to make the best possible presentation, give both sides of the picture— before someone else has the chance to jump on your interpretation and destroy it.

Suppose you seek approval of increased payroll budget in

your department. To balance that, you intend to prove—through analysis—that you can *save* the company money by eliminating overhead, upgrading internal systems, and eliminating expensive, outdated equipment.

You know that the accountant will object to a higher salary budget, since your expenses have been rising for the past two years. And last year, expenses exceeded your budget considerably. So as part of your report, you present the information you know the accountant would present if given the chance. In this way, you effectively take away the best arguments *against* your ideas. You also present yourself as an individual who is not afraid to present the full picture, including information going against what you want.

Sometimes you might not be sure what your analysis means. This trend might be inconclusive, or the direction of the trend might not be clear enough to define its meaning. In this situation, the best approach is to offer two or more *likely* meanings. State your opinion as to which is most likely, but present all the possibilities of which you are aware. Give others the chance to draw their own conclusions from your data.

If you don't know what the trend reveals, don't make any conclusive statements. Promise to get more information and report back. Ask for help when you need it. Use available resources and—most of all—consult with the people involved.

Remember these important points about presenting your findings:

• **Look beyond the obvious.** Don't assume that a trend means what it appears to mean in every case, just because it looks the same as another trend you have studied previously. It could be that a less than obvious answer contradicts your obvious answer.

• **Check with the people involved and affected.** This point is extremely important. Whenever you plan to present an interpretation of a trend, first check with the people that are affected. You cannot afford the wrath of a divisional vice president or a department manager who is called to account for a problem without being warned ahead of time. This is especially true if your interpretation is wrong!

• **When you're not sure, say so.** The only unforgivable sin is failing to say that you don't know. You will not be judged harshly for not having the answers, unless you try to convince others that you do. Get your facts and go into meetings (or submit reports) as fully prepared as possible, and with as many questions anticipated and answered in advance. When unexpected questions arise, or when you can't find the answers, say so directly.

Best-Case and Worst-Case Reporting

Some trends may reveal a general direction and a generally good or bad outcome, but you still cannot pin down the precise meaning of the trend, at least not to the degree you would like. In these instances, you might need to report what is known as a best-case or worst-case outcome; that is, a range of probable outcomes revealed by the trend.

> *Example:* You have prepared a preliminary budget for your department. Two very large expense categories were budgeted on the basis of your study of the past two years. However, because the range of estimated expenses is fairly large, you cannot precisely arrive at a reasonable budget from this information alone. So instead of presenting one budget result, you give two: the best case (lowest overall outcome) and worst case (highest overall outcome).

Presenting a likely range is not popular with decision makers. They want you to narrow down the range to one number. One alternative is to find secondary information from other sources that might either confirm or deny what your own trend analysis showed. They might narrow down the range, or give you an alternative method for arriving at a reasonable and supportable answer.

> *Example:* You presented your budget for two categories of expenses, using best-case and worst-case summaries. However,

now you need to narrow the range into one budget number. Since the work of your department is directly affected by activity in marketing, you get a copy of the marketing department moving average for volume of new orders per month, and develop your budget based on the marketing department's estimated trend. As long as those results fall within the range you developed on your own, you calculate that it is fair to budget on that basis. If the outcome falls outside your range, you adjust it to the highest or lowest point within the range.

In this example, two carefully developed but independent studies were applied to budget the future. This is entirely appropriate as long as both studies were accurate and as long as there is some connection between the two.

THE QUESTION OF PROFIT

How do you go into a meeting to present your analysis concerning the most intangible issue, and still address the issue of profit? What if your topic has nothing at all to do with profits? The fact is, every business issue is involved directly with the question of profits. If the problem does not involve increasing sales or profits directly, or reducing costs or expenses, it has to do with a secondary issue that *does* have a profit side. With this reality always at the front of your mind, your approach during the meeting—to everything you hear as well as in all that you say—should be to ask and then answer these questions about profit:

• **How will the decision increase or decrease profits?** Every decision involves a question about profits. That defines the risk involved, and explains why decisions are so difficult to make. Decision makers must contend with the risk that their decision will reduce profits rather than increase or maintain them.

If you ask this question when presenting information, you make the decision maker's job much easier. By providing the answers, you are more likely to gain the decision you want. You have already done the job for the other person.

• **What alternatives would be more cost effective?** Never close your mind to the possibility that the solution you propose is not the best one. Someone else might have alternatives for you to consider, that are more cost effective, more efficient, or easier to put into action. Ask yourself this question constantly. It helps you keep your mind clear and open, and prevents you from failing to see what might be obvious to another person.

• **Is the timing good, or would it be more profitable to wait?** In some cases, the idea you present is a good one, but the timing is poor. Any number of outside influences can affect timing, such as strong competition or seasonal factors. Perhaps top management is contending with a serious cash flow problem. For whatever reasons, if your idea is turned down, don't give up. If you still believe the idea has merit, present it again a few months later. In many cases, the second try will lead to a different outcome.

• **What additional information do we need to make this decision?** Here's a question the decision maker is constantly asking. So if you ask it first, you will prevent delays. Anticipate, plan, and deliver the results the executive needs and wants. Look at your own presentation with a fresh eye. How have you presented your facts? Is it objective? Do you address the other point of view? Have you examined arguments against your proposal and explained where they are flawed? Most of all, have you demonstrated how your idea lowers risk and increases profits?

• **What extra steps can we take today to make the outcome more profitable?** Even when your idea is received with enthusiasm, it might only be the first step. Look ahead and decide what has to be done to take advantage of the idea, to expand it beyond its first stage. Assume you'll get approval. What has to happen next to exploit the go-ahead and increase profits even more?

MAKING YOUR POINT WITH ANALYSIS

Let's assume the best case: You attend meetings that are well organized, with a prepublished agenda; they are led by a capable leader who can make decisions; and every participant takes part with great enthusiasm and effectiveness. Even in this ideal situation, where others listen to you with complete and pure motives, and where political motive or thought doesn't apply, you still need to make your case and prove your point. That requires the presentation of facts with certain attributes suitable for the busy decision maker:

• **The case must be presented clearly.** Presentations given in a meeting are generally oral. If any written material is given out, it's usually just supporting material. Rarely will you just give out a report and let it speak for itself; you will be asked to stand up and make a presentation.

The first rule: State your case clearly. Don't start with a series of explanations about how your analysis was prepared. Begin by saying what it proves. State the conclusion and then work backward, explaining why and how that's the case. Make your point clearly and simply. Even then, expect questions and be ready to repeat and clarify again.

• **Key facts should be summarized at the top.** When you make your presentation, always start out with the key facts. This might include a summary of the problem your analysis addresses; a promise to deliver a solution with a proposal you want to make; or the conclusions you came to as the result of analysis for a project you were assigned at the last meeting.

The point here: Don't waste the time of others in the meeting. Get right to the important information they want to hear. Begin with the most critical conclusion, and then back into the less important issues. Assume that you could be interrupted and told to sit down at any moment. This technique forces you to arrange information with the highest priority expressed first, and that's the best way to make your presentation.

• **Recommendations are always welcome.** Many people go into meetings and give meek, passive reports, afraid to come out and say what the company should do. In fact, decision makers prefer reports that include specific recommendations. Otherwise, they only get raw information, and are forced to interpret everything on their own.

You have put in the time and effort to research the problem and its solutions. *You* are the expert. Don't be afraid to make a suggestion, even a bold one. Tell the decision maker *how* to solve a problem, and you will make a very favorable impression. You make the decision maker's task easier, and you will get your way more often. That's the key that many overlook.

• **Details should be provided, but only as back matter.** You prepare your presentation with full awareness that your facts will be questioned, so you have a lot of detailed worksheets available. But they clutter your presentation and your mind, you end up buried in your own statistics.

The solution: Keep the presentation brief and clean. Have the supporting documentation at hand, and be prepared to refer to it, but don't bring it out unless you have to. In some cases, you will want to compile a cross-reference section of supporting information, and supply the package to everyone in the meeting. It's more likely that you won't be asked to provide that level of detail, as others are usually too busy to audit your claims and your information. But someone might ask you where you got your numbers, especially if they don't believe your conclusions or like your recommendations. Make your point by having the proof ready.

Some guidelines for preparing yourself to report with confidence:

• **Practice file organization and cross-referencing techniques.** Having a good filing system helps increase confidence in yourself and your numbers. Being able to find what you need as quickly as possible makes a good impression on others. The file itself is not the goal, but a well-organized filing and cross-referencing system is a considerable advantage, especially if you have a lot of paperwork. Imagine a file of forty to fifty worksheets and other supporting documents. You *will* need to organize that mess in some way, if you ever hope to locate the one worksheet you need to answer a tough question from a decision maker.

• **Rehearse your presentation.** If you are already familiar with your material, you don't generally need to rehearse before presenting the report. But when you will be using a lot of cross-reference material, it makes sense to be sure you will be able to find things you will need during your presentation. Rehearsal might help overcome technical problems that could arise during the presentation. Run through your material, laying out the details of your report. Arrange supporting documentation so that the materials most likely to be needed are close at hand. Then provide yourself with secondary cross-reference to other materials you might need.

• **Get an ally in the audience.** Find one person who will be at the meeting who endorses your point of view. Go through your report with that person and, when making the presentation, you will know you have that ally in the room. It could make a tremendous difference.

• **Be prepared for any question—even the one you don't know how to answer.** A prepared speaker has answers to all the questions it would be reasonable to ask. If you are familiar with your material, you already know what is likely to be on the minds of other people in the meeting. But even the most prepared presenter can't anticipate every possible question. If you don't know the answer, say so, but promise to find the answer and report back as soon as possible. If you think it will take an hour to find the answer, promise to respond within two hours; if you think it will take half a day, promise an answer in one day. Then come through as promised, without fail. If for any reason you're unable to get the answer to the person by the promised time, get in touch, explain the problem, and give a new deadline. Also send a copy of the memo answering the question to everyone else in attendance at the meeting. Get the reputation as someone who keeps promises.

CHARTING THE TREND

Once you have identified the best possible method of summarizing the information under study, you next need to select a reporting method. This is where many people, even capable analysts, miss the point. Unfortunately, it is possible to get very close to a completely effective trend report, only to forget one point: Your audience still needs to have the facts reduced to a comprehensible form.

The best way to report anything numerical is with visual aids. You can list a series of ratios in a neat column, and your audience will quickly lose interest. Or you can show the same information on a graph. The curve of change, especially if two related factors are being compared, is then extremely visual.

Visual aids are powerful tools for making your point. You can talk all day about how your ideas have improved efficiency and profits, without results. A simple graph, however, may speak for you with much greater power. Some guidelines for using visual aids are listed below and are summarized in Figure 11-2:

• **Label everything correctly and clearly.** Graphics are meant to clarify, to bring an otherwise obscure series of facts into focus. The observer should be able to tell immediately what the graphic shows, and what it means. For example, if a graph contains information on two related financial outcomes, that should be apparent immediately. If you need to explain what a graphic shows, then it probably needs clearer labeling.

• **Annotate, footnote, or include legends.** Labels don't always provide all the information an audience should have. Special situations require extra labeling. For example, an extraordinary item that causes a glitch in a trend could be annotated off to the side. Or a footnote could be provided to explain or clarify a point. Legends are especially useful when a visual aid contains two or more pieces of information, or when two different scales are being used.

• **Keep it very simple.** Don't make the mistake of trying to

Figure 11-2.   Guidelines: using visual aids.

1. Label everything correctly and clearly.

2. Annotate, footnote, or include legends.

3. Keep it very simple.

4. Make sure the scale is right.

5. Keep the same scale for all related graphics.

6. Place graphics as close as possible to related text.

7. Don't waste time explaining what the graph already shows.

include everything on one graphic. If you have two different but related outcomes, you can put them together on one page, and the whole picture will be clear. But if you try to crowd four or five different outcomes on one graphic, you could run into problems.

• **Make sure the scale is right.** As a general rule, your graphic representation of a trend analysis should be square or slightly rectangular; this is a pleasing shape for an observer. If the shape of your graphic is odd or awkward, the meaningful information contained within it will be lost. The shape of a graphic is controlled through the selection of scale. For example, breaking down the top-to-bottom values by $25,000 increments might make the graph too high; but breaking it out by $100,000 increments might make it just right. And time values, going from left to right, can be increased, reduced, or spread out to accommodate the more desirable square or rectangular shape.

• **Keep the same scale for all related graphics.** Selection of scale isn't always isolated to one graphic. You might have a series of related graphics that deal with similar information. In this case, select a scale that is suitable for all. Be sure to keep the same scale in effect for each graphic.

• **Place graphics as close as possible to related text.** In a written report, place all graphic material as close as possible to the applicable section of the report. This is critical. To gain maximum value, the audience should be able to see the graphic as they're reading and thinking about the underlying issue. Some reports include all graphic material in an appendix. This requires flipping back and forth to find each graphic; in the process, comprehension slips away.

• **Don't waste time explaining what the graph already shows.** In the text of the report, emphasize the interpretive. Make recommendations. Talk about action and the future. Don't repeat what the graph already demonstrates clearly. The real value of visual aids is that they replace the need to write explanations of numbers, leaving you room to show the outcomes.

Chapter 12

Using Analysis in Reports

The day will arrive when you, the nonaccountant manager, have to confront a meeting room full of executives and accountants. It's natural to feel at a disadvantage, especially if you're there to talk about the numbers.

Your success will depend on your own attitude, the amount of research and preparation, and internal factors of personalities and company politics. When you decide to take the analytical approach and use skills that accountants use, you will meet with one of two responses from the accountants. In a highly political, negative environment, you will be perceived as a personal threat and your ideas will be met with resistance, even hostility. In a more enlightened company, your new ideas will be seen as a refreshing change.

So there you are, at the presentation end of the table. You open your file, take out your report, and begin distributing copies. No one is smiling. In fact, as the accountant begins to read, a deep frown comes across his face. You begin. You carefully explain your premise and assumptions. A few questions are asked, and you answer promptly. There's a moment of uncomfortable silence. Then the president, at the far end of the table, asks, "Are there any more questions?" When there's no response, he nods at you and says, "All right, let's do it."

This is one scenario. However, it is a sad reality that some of the most dynamic and talented analysts are never able to make their talent known. If they are unable to convey their information to others, it cannot be used in a worthwhile manner. Mastering the analysis itself is only part of the task. You also need to find ways to communicate what you have learned. And that usually means writing and presenting a report.

Do your reports get read? Or are they merely filed away with the others and left to take up space? A meeting at the very least involves interaction between people; reports are not even necessarily looked at. And when they are, there's no guarantee that the reader will respond to you. Many a report has been quietly dropped into a garbage can, regardless of how valuable the information might be.

The problem here is not just that your careful and detailed analysis will be wasted. The greater risk is that important issues won't be acted upon. Your profit-oriented ideas and recommendations could be bypassed, merely because the right people didn't read your report. You can overcome these risks and make sure your analysis does get the attention it deserves. I propose a new method for presenting reports, which is built on one unavoidable fact: The busy decision maker doesn't want to take the time to wade through a lengthy document. Make it easy for that decision maker to find answers quickly, preferably by looking on the first page only.

A NEW REPORTING METHOD

Think about most of the reports you have seen. They have no design and no format. Information just piles up, page after page, more or less in the order it came up. Another trait of the typical report is that little if anything conclusive is in it. Or, if it is, it's difficult to find. Conclusions are scattered throughout, cryptically disguised as narrative amid other narrative sections. There is no road map to follow, not even a table of contents in the front. And when you do read through a complete section, you might not even be sure what it says.

It doesn't take much to solve the common problems found in reports. Highlight your conclusions. Boldly draw attention to them. That's the entire purpose of doing the report: to present ideas and solutions based on facts and study, and then to compel response and action. Some ideas for improving reports are listed below and summarized in Figure 12-1:

• **Make the report informative.** All too often, reports are done only because they are supposed to be. The deadline is imposed, you comply. The finished report is sent to a distribution list and filed. No one questions it or responds. You probably suspect that no one even reads it.

The problem is the way reports are originated. A one-time assignment gives the decision maker something of value, so someone decides to continue the report month after month.

Figure 12-1. Guidelines: improving your reports.

1. Make the report informative.

2. Make the report interesting.

3. Make it easy to find the information.

4. Put your conclusions together in one place.

5. Forget about old designs.

6. Write with extreme clarity.

7. Place graphics with narrative discussions.

8. Suggest cancelling some recurring reports.

No one reads it, but the idea of abandoning the report never comes up.

Overcome this problem by making your report valuable. Don't accept the fact that passive reporting is the way of the corporate world. Change things. Point out the value in your report, and ask for specific responses from people on your distribution list.

• **Make the report interesting.** Few people seem to know how to make reports interesting. In fact, the very idea is surprising to many old hands, because they've never seen an interesting report yet. Attempt to convey your own enthusiasm in the way you express ideas. What is interesting about your analysis? What shocking or surprising facts did you uncover?

• **Make it easy to find the information.** In typical report design, information is thrown together in seemingly haphazard fashion. You might be very familiar with a body of facts, but try to remember that people on your distribution list will probably be seeing it for the first time. Give your readers a little guidance. Tell them where to find things. Label sections clearly so that they have an idea of the subject being discussed. Use subheads, especially for longer sections. Number the pages throughout the report and include a table of contents. This takes a few minutes to prepare but makes the report much easier to read.

• **Put your conclusions together in one place.** Imagine receiving a forty-page report with urgent information included. You're a busy executive, rushing to the board meeting. You have to wade through the entire report just to find one or two numbers you must have at once.

Unfortunately, this is typical. Make your reports much more valuable by putting all your conclusions together in one place. Make it easy for the reader to find the summary of what you're trying to convey. Then back up that summarized information with detailed sections of the report.

• **Forget about old designs.** Why are reports prepared in specific though limiting formats? Because that's how they've always been done. But that doesn't mean you *must* live with it.

In fact, that could be the best reason to enact a change as quickly as possible.

Make a change that works. Try altering the format of a report that's difficult to read or follow. Come up with a new design that makes it easy for someone to get through it quickly. Assume that all the people on your distribution list will give your report about two minutes of attention, and you'll be just about right. When they turn to page one, what do you want them to read?

• **Write with extreme clarity.** Clear writing is brief. You don't need to fill up many pages when a few pages will suffice. If last month's report was thirty-eight pages, that doesn't mean this month's version has to be at least as long. Try to make it shorter. You might be able to cover the same ground in fewer than ten pages.

Corporate writing gets out of hand because so many people assume it has to follow a certain style. But in fact, we all appreciate reading something that's written in a friendly, conversational tone. Small words do work better than larger ones that mean the same thing. And when you come right out and say what you mean with extreme clarity, that's better than hedging and moving around the statement without ever making it.

• **Place graphics with narrative discussions.** In too many reports, charts and graphs are dumped together in the last section. Readers are constantly stopping to find the applicable graphic, flipping pages back and forth. If you want your reports to have value to readers, assume that they will comprehend what you're saying only if you make it easy for them. Graphics help comprehension, but be sure to place them near the related discussion, on the same page if possible.

• **Suggest cancelling some recurring reports.** Here's the most shocking idea of all: canceling a report that's always been done. You want your analysis to be given the attention it deserves, but what you're hearing over and over is the same argument. There's too much information coming in, and no time to read it.

The reason: Everyone is preparing reports on a variety of subjects, and all the file space in the company is being taken up with information no one ever looks at again. It might just be possible to stop doing some of those reports. Some suggestions you can make include reducing the frequency of reports (from monthly to quarterly, for example), reducing the scope of a report, cutting back on the distribution list, or eliminating it altogether.

When you encounter resistance to this idea, ask the other people if they even need the report. The answer will probably be, "I don't look at it, but I might need to one day." Assure them that, if the information is ever needed, you will be glad to supply it. With this approach, you might just be able to do away with some reports that now take up a lot of your time.

ADDING MEANING TO THE NUMBERS

There is a very large gap between meekly handing over a report, and telling someone else what it means. There is a big difference between reporting a column of numbers, and recommending action. These differences mark the distinction between merely complying with a request, and creatively assuming a leadership role. A leader looks beyond the surface of the request, anticipates the decision maker's needs and answers them, and constantly strives to improve the bottom line.

The typical financial reports given to decision makers are among the most passive forms of reporting. Yet, they are widely accepted as the norm. Some well-known examples:

- The accountant submits a set of financial statements to the finance committee; the only comments included are the standard footnotes.
- Department and division managers compare actual costs and expenses to the monthly budget; comments are offered as to the causes of unfavorable variances, but no action is recommended and none is taken.

- A department manager prepares an account analysis every month for several active accounts; however, no one on the distribution list does anything with the report beyond filing it.

In each instance, the effort is put forward and nothing comes from it. So how can you add real meaning to the numbers on such reports? How can you make your analysis stand out from the rest? Here are some guidelines:

- **Don't report the numbers. Provide solutions to the problems at issue.** A report should do more than just list information. It should *report* that information in a meaningful way. If you were entrusted with preparation of the report, you should assume the role of an expert. Management believes in you enough to have given you the job. Now do it. Instead of just listing out the numbers that respond to the obvious question (as everyone else does), ask yourself what problem the decision maker wants to solve. Why does the decision maker want this information? If you don't know, ask. Then prepare a report that solves the problem and shows the way to higher profits, less risk, less complication. That's what makes analysis valuable, and that's also what makes you shine as a manager.

- **Don't settle for the norm. Constantly look for a better way to report.** People get very frustrated when they inherit a reporting function. The format might be overly complex, or unnecessarily broad. Don't just accept these problems; solve them. Suggest a simplified format, one that requires less time and effort, but gives the recipient more information.

- **When conventional forces oppose you, speak out. Suggest change. Show others the illogic of the status quo.** Never settle for the explanation, "But that's the way we've always done it." That is the worst reason to not institute a change. All too often, the status quo does not work well, it costs too much, and it doesn't solve problems. Suggest a change. If that isn't acceptable, propose using a dual procedure for a couple of months, then suggest going with the method that works best.

• **Try something new.** It's sometimes worth the effort to shake up the routine. See if you can raise some dust in the corporate hallway by trying something new. It doesn't have to be radically new or threatening, especially if it's also expensive, just something new and experimental. The more conservative types in your company need to be reminded that they *can* survive a new idea.

BEGIN WITH THE CONCLUSION

Look at your reports from the readers' point of view. Can they find information quickly and efficiently? Can they get the key ideas without having to read all the supporting material?

Above all else, reports should be easy to use. Put your most important information on page one. State the problem the report addresses, then list the conclusions you reached. End the page with your recommendations for action. That summary page is the most valuable part of the report. The reader can look it over in a few moments and can quickly refer to those sections of the report that support your claims. The conclusions should be cross-referenced to specific pages to make this possible.

To make your reports valuable to everyone on your distribution list:

• Make your reports so practical that they will be remembered.
• State conclusions boldly and in absolute terms, but be certain that you are right.
• In the detailed sections, explain your proof in terms of analysis. Show that you are capable of working with financial information.
• Strive for absolute clarity. Don't complicate, simplify.

The busy reader whose time is always at a premium will remember your format above all others. You will also find that executives call on you when they want hard information. Your internal influence will rise as your reports are distributed.

Incorporate the "conclusion first" style in other forms of communication. When you're asked to make a presentation in a meeting, start out by listing your conclusions. Then fill in details as needed, or answer questions from others in attendance. You will find this to be one of the most effective methods for conveying information and ideas to others. The key is that you are able to back up your conclusions with proof.

REPORTING WITH CONFIDENCE

When you learn to incorporate analysis into your reports, your confidence level will increase noticeably. This change comes about because you are using the same skills accountants practice as a matter of routine. There is an appropriate level of influence connected with reporting in a thoroughly documented and proof-oriented manner. You deserve the respect and confidence of others, because you have learned to use those skills.

Accountants are able to report their facts with complete confidence, because they know their numbers are correct. All the accounting systems and procedures in use are designed to check and double-check accuracy. You need and want the same level of integrity in your facts and figures. That involves gathering proof, and then arranging it so that it can be located quickly. You may need, for example, to organize your own notes and files so that questions can be fielded with relative ease. That way, when you are asked to prove your point, you can go directly to the proof without having to fumble through piles of papers.

Whether your report is written or oral, the reporting format will reflect your sense of organization. In those cases where you enter a meeting, pass out a written report, and then give an oral presentation to the other attendees, this well-organized filing system is critical. This format is the most effective means for delivering a report; it is also the most potentially threatening, since you must be well organized in order to make a favorable impression.

NARRATIVE EXPLANATIONS

In preparing your report, remember that no one enjoys reading about numbers. The narrative sections of the report are the parts people will read, especially if they hope to gain information from what you have done. To make your analysis worth their time, follow the guidelines listed below and summarized in Figure 12-2:

• **Use active voice.** People respond well to active-voice writing, but they fall asleep when they're forced to read endless passive statements. You have probably seen the following type of statement numerous times: "It is the task of each manager to ensure that deadlines are met." That's passive voice. It would be better to say, "Managers should ensure that

Figure 12-2. Guidelines: writing narrative sections.

1. Use active voice.

2. Avoid saying the obvious.

3. Talk about what the numbers show.

4. Let the numbers speak for themselves.

5. Avoid the need for explanation by using ratios.

deadlines are met." It's shorter, clearer, and easier to understand. Use the active voice throughout your report. If you are
in the habit of reporting in the passive voice, make it a personal
project to change your style. Passive voice *is* the common
business language, especially in reporting. That's why so much
of what you're forced to read is dull.

• **Avoid saying the obvious.** Another common flaw in
reports is to state the obvious. This takes up space and puts
the reader to sleep. For example, in budget reports, you often
see explanations of variances like this: "The office supply
expense has exceeded the budget." That's not really an explanation at all. It is a waste of space that would be better used to
describe the *reason* for the variance. Analysis must reveal information, or it is not truly analysis. Assign yourself a space
budget for your report. Stay within that budget and cut out
anything that the reader already knows or can see just by
looking at the numbers. Another idea: Write the report once,
then go through and try to say the same thing in half the
space. You'll be surprised at how this forces you to write
concisely.

• **Talk about what the numbers show.** Perhaps the dullest
writing is that which simply repeats what the numbers already
show. To avoid this, place the numbers on the same page as
the explanation, box them off, and then spend your energy
interpreting them. It's much more valuable to explain what the
numbers reveal, than to simply list them in a different version.

• **Let the numbers speak for themselves.** Another option
is to say nothing about the numbers. Don't feel compelled to
provide analysis or interpretation, or to indicate a trend, if you
really have nothing to say about the numbers.

• **Avoid the need for explanation by using ratios.** Financial
ratios can help you clarify the point, and then you don't have
to contend with the numbers directly. For example, suppose
you are preparing a report that summarizes a manufacturing
shift's efforts at reducing defective parts. You observe a decline
to a point, and then a leveling off. The level is acceptable, and
that's the point you want to make in your report. By way of

proof, however, you could list out the entire history of your analysis, or you could summarize by using ratios instead.

WRITING REPORTS THAT GET USED

When you think about a busy executive reading reports, memos, letters, and other written communications, you will realize that time is extremely valuable. You do a service to that executive when you're able to put forth a lot of information in a very brief space. No one enjoys reading through a ninety-page report—especially if they receive little useful information. A solution is to break down your report into three sections:

1. Summary page. Put your major findings and recommendations on a single page, and make that the first page of your report. This enables readers to see the whole report in a minute or two. If they want more information, they can refer to sections two or three.

2. Narrative sections. The second section is the body of the report. It includes narrative sections and any graphics or other related material. Include graphic information within the narrative sections, rather than in an appendix. This makes the report easier to comprehend.

3. Detailed support. Behind the narrative section, you may include copies of worksheets, calculations, computer printouts, and any other backup information that proves your case. This detailed support section will help you provide answers to questions that may come up.

Make a clear distinction between these three sections. Avoid preparing passive reports that just go from one page to another, without any real focus.

Also make sure you provide a mechanism to help readers find the proof they might need. For example, an executive is reading the analysis narrative, where you claim the trend proves your point. She wants to see more. You need to direct her attention to a worksheet somewhere in the detailed report section, but how? Two methods are suggested: footnotes and individual citation.

A *footnote* is given at the bottom of the page where the topic first appears. Refer to a specific page in your detailed analysis section. You should number *all* pages of your report, and include a table of contents for any report longer than ten pages. In the footnote, give the title of the worksheet or printout, and the page number where it can be found.

A *citation* presents your source for a key point, without forcing the reader to look elsewhere. In the citation, you quote from another report, a printout, or other source, or you reproduce a summary of your own analysis. Put it at the bottom of the page or on the next page.

NEW FORMATS AND APPROACHES

It might be entirely appropriate for you to replace one report format with another. If a format is not working, it is time to come up with something better, and it is your job to improve on reporting and communication methods. You will probably run into a lot of resistance. It's human nature to resist change. To convince others that your ideas make sense, try these approaches:

• **Point out profitable features.** Your readers will be most responsive to the idea that a new format will save money. Point out that the report now takes one person three days, and your revised format can be done in less than half that time. Calculate the monthly and annual savings, and provide the decision maker with some hard dollar amounts.

• **Suggest a dual report for one or two months.** People resist change because of fear—they are afraid to take the risk of allowing change. Your solution is to relieve the fear. Suggest doing the report for one or two months in both formats. If yours is truly better, then your readers will gravitate to it. You will make your point and the change will be allowed to happen.

- **Make the change without asking permission.** The most efficient way to make change occur is to take action on your own, if you can. Remember, if you've been given responsibility for doing a report each month, you *are* the expert. You have a lot to say about the report's content and format. When others notice the change and comment upon it, all you need to say is that the new format is more efficient and practical than the old one. Say it with confidence, and your change will likely be accepted.

Chapter 13

Analysis as a Problem-Solving Tool

We tend to think of financial analysis as belonging only in the realm of accounting. But in fact, we all have to perform many accounting functions, and no one has an exclusive on the numbers or on their interpretation. Analysis is nothing more than a tool for solving problems and devising solutions. You can make a point if your facts are arranged with financial considerations at the very front. Communicating these facts in ways used by accountants makes sense. When information is presented in the familiar format, people understand it better. Decision makers respond best to arguments aimed at the bottom line. Remember, too, that *you* are the most qualified to do your particular analysis. In matters affecting your department, you are the expert.

TRAINING YOUR EMPLOYEES

Your use of analysis as a problem-solving tool does not have to be limited to meetings and reports. You can also help your own employees to think in more advanced terms. Staff members become more valuable to you once you train them in the proper use of analysis. You can do this by showing them how to take a different approach to solving problems.

Example: An employee in your department knocks on your door one morning and enters your office. He begins at once to complain about the antiquated typewriter he uses to type up reports. "I really need a new machine now," he whines. "Why don't you buy me one?"

This is a terrific opportunity for coaching. First, you want to help the employee get what he wants—if it is appropriate. Second, you want to show him how to ask for something without creating resistance. Cooperation works much better.

Example: Explain your problem to the employee. You work with a limited budget, and employee demands for solutions only make your job harder. "The best way to get what you want," you say, "is to figure out your own solution and then put it on my desk. Make my job easier. Show me how buying you a new typewriter will save money for the department. Then you'll have my attention."

A manager is expected to see things more clearly and from a higher viewpoint. Teaching your staff to analyze intelligently is a worthwhile investment, if only because it makes your job easier. It provides much more, of course. The employee who understands how to ask for something (by demonstrating that a positive response means higher profits) is more valuable to you and to the company. That individual is constantly looking for opportunities to improve profits—and that's every employee's job.

SETTING DEPARTMENTAL AND PERSONAL GOALS

Analysis is not just a way to master the complexities of financial information. It is also an excellent tool for setting goals on many levels, tracking them, and creating a higher ratio of success.

Departmental goals are perfectly suited for analysis, since

they often are expressed in numerical terms. The departmental goal, by nature, is expressed in the budget. Analysis of numerical information fits the budgeting format, and is easily monitored through the variance tracking and explanation system.

Personal goals may be harder to identify through the process of analysis, because people rarely express their goals in financial terms. Someone might say he wants to make a certain salary, but that's probably only part of the real underlying goal. It's more likely that the employee's goal will relate to career advancement.

> The sign of a keen and talented analyst is the ability to translate intangibles and, in the process, identify the real goal and purpose even when it has not been stated.

PASSIVE AND ACTIVE REPORTING

One of the flaws in the accountant's world is that the "product" that comes from every effort is financial. That means that even the most abstract of issues is always reflected in terms of profit and loss. And if the reporting procedures are passive, then few people will appreciate what reports reveal. Even when negative trends are shown, the passive system means that no action will be taken.

There is nothing much you can do to change the way accounting departments prepare their information. However, you can change the way you relate to financial information. It means moving from a passive posture to a more active stance. Some ideas:

• **Change tradition in your own department.** You might be frustrated in attempts to gain more information than someone else is willing to provide. However, you can make a difference in the way you report *your* own information.

Insist on giving active reports. Provide information and recommendations for action that will improve profits or reduce expenses. No matter what someone else asks for, give them the profit orientation you assume they really want. When you prepare reports, always include suggestions and recommendations, even if you're not asked.

• **Invite questions and provide answers in anticipation of unspoken ones.** Never be afraid of being questioned by others, in meetings or in one-to-one discussion. Even when questions are asked with hostility, confront the issues rather than the people. Let personal feelings and reactions go to the side, and deal with the issues directly.

When you prepare reports or make presentations, try to anticipate what others want. Provide answers before the hard questions are asked. And whenever possible, raise the issues that go against what your report claims. Be willing to deal with those issues even if it poses a threat to the recommendations you're making.

• **Ask the right questions in meetings.** When you attend meetings called by other people, ask the right questions. For example, if the accountant presents a balance sheet and income statement, ask some pointed questions. What is the trend in profits for the year? Is it favorable? How does it compare to last year? Is working capital adequate for the upcoming busy season? If not, what capitalization alternatives is the accountant exploring? What areas should be improved upon in budgeting and forecasting? What specific ideas does the accountant have? What actions should be taken now, and by whom, to put those ideas into effect?

Chapter 14

When the Numbers Don't Help

If you have met very many accountants, auditors, or other financial experts, you already know that the numbers are not the whole story. When people place all their emphasis just on the numbers, they communicate poorly and seem to not understand the human side of any issues.

Unfortunately, some of the stereotyping from which the accountant suffers is caused by a tendency to relate better to numbers than to people. The truly talented accountant recognizes that all issues are, in fact, human (although they have a financial side); and that using numbers to make a point is of limited value within the more human context of the issue.

This rule applies to all departments equally. The pure sales personality might do well to realize that there is more to life than closing the sale. The customer service expert might be better rounded by admitting that, contrary to the traditional belief, the customer is *not* always right. And the busy executive will be more effective by stopping now and then to chat with someone from the mailroom.

Everyone can enrich their corporate perspectives by looking at issues from another person's point of view. When it comes to analysis, you should realize that there are cases where the numbers don't improve your argument, increase your influence, or change someone else's mind.

THE IMPORTANCE OF INTUITION

The more experienced you are as an employee, the more valuable your intuition becomes. Intuition guides us and helps us sort through infinite choices and alternatives. Only when we narrow down those choices can we apply the more analytical skills we might possess. The best of both worlds is to pay heed to your intuition, and to then go forth and prove your point scientifically.

Pure analysis (science) and hunch (intuition) are not dissimilar skills. They are only different aspects of the same thing, which is the sum and whole of your knowledge and experience. You cannot ignore the need for either side, and your goal might be to make the two work together better. The scientific mind can grant even a limited amount of respect to the intuitive; and the intuitive side can admit that proof is, indeed, helpful in winning influence and getting decision makers to go along with ideas.

In the corporate world, experience is usually given more respect than intuition is. You can use intuition, but it might be unwise to admit that you're making recommendations on that basis. Even if you depend largely on "subconscious experience" to advise the decision makers in your company, it's wise to back up your ideas with the proof you develop through analysis. In this way, you satisfy your own hunches, while conforming to the corporate bias against intuition as a skill worth listening to.

You gain respect and influence not by title, but by the nature and quality of the work you do. It's just a matter of proving, through consistent output, that you are dependable, and that your analytical insights deserve the decision maker's attention.

You do not need to become an accountant to achieve this result. All you need to do is learn to apply the same skills and procedures they use. That, combined with the fact that you are already an expert in your own department and understand issues far beyond the numbers, makes you a powerful management force in your company—a force that knows how to convey ideas and present facts accurately and truthfully.

Index

[Italicized numbers indicate figures.]